JAN 3, 2012

FLORIDA

ESCAMBIA

SANTA ROSA

OKALOOSA

WALTON

BAY

PANAMA CITY

PENSACOLA

GULF

FRANKLIN

MEXICO

APALACHICOLA

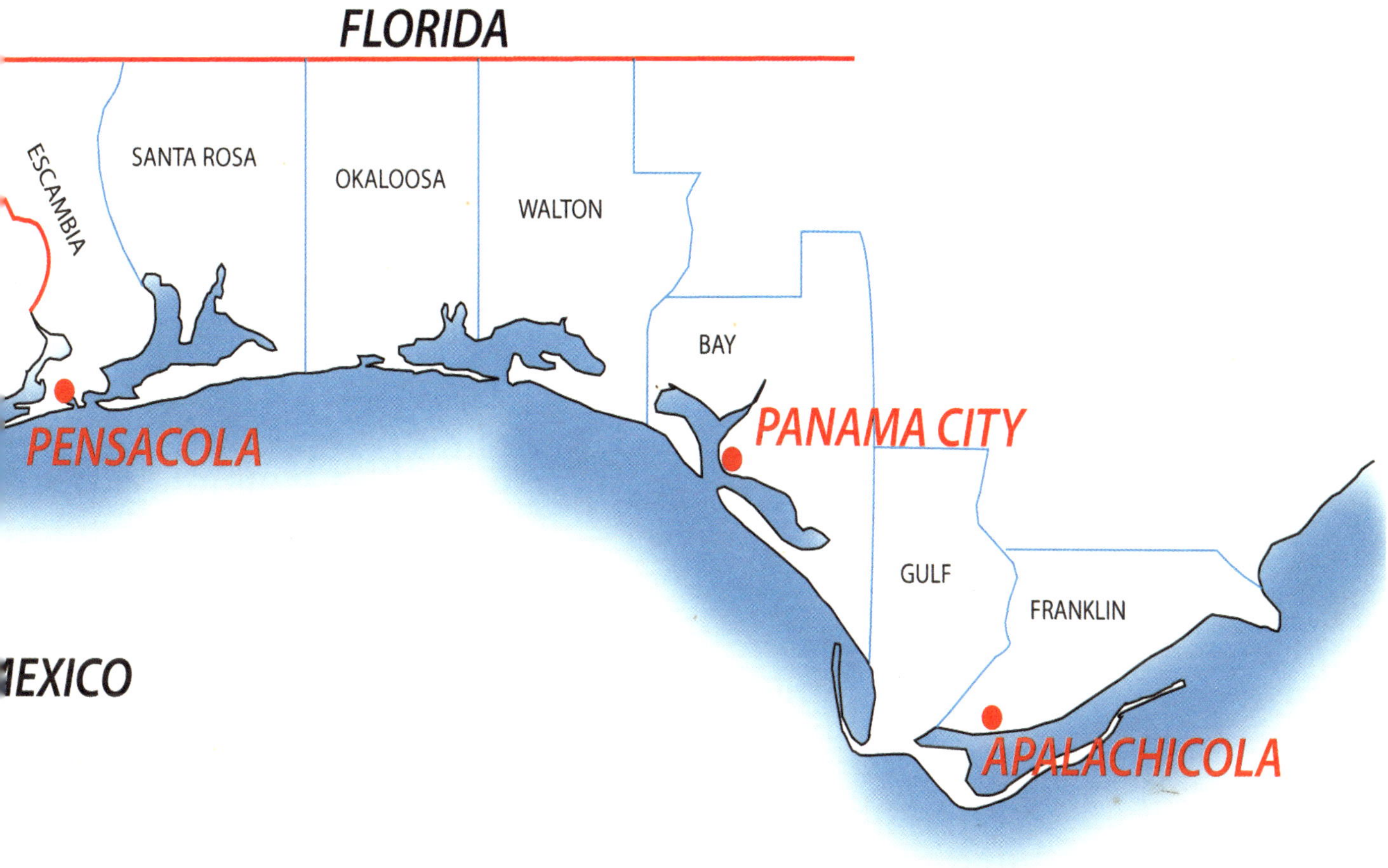

The Gulf Coast Landscape

From Apalachicola to New Orleans

A Primer for New Home Owners

by Mike Robertson

Cover Photo: Morning Glory volunteers to enhance an architectural feature of a historic building on the waterfront in Apalachicola, Florida. Nature is extraordinary.

ISBN: 978-1-934035-84-9

Trent's Prints and Publishing
Pace, Florida
Printed in the United States of America

We come from the earth.

We return to the earth.

In between, we garden.

Author unknown

Table of Contents

ACKNOWLEDGMENTS

For an entire year, I worked on my concept of this book. Articles that I had written, along with outlines of talks that I had given were collected, refined and organized. Over the subsequent year, the chapters were arranged and reorganized. Trips were taken to gather photographs in different parts of the Gulf Coast, in different seasons. My wife, Darcy, took over a thousand photographs on these journeys. They were pleasant journeys. The Gulf Coast is inviting and exciting. We stayed on the tranquil shores of St. Joe Bay near the eastern end of our Gulf Coast, and in the bustling city of New Orleans on the western end. But no matter where we were photographing plants and landscapes, we always felt as though we were home. That is one of the most charming aspects of the Gulf Coast. It always feels like home.

Darcy also typed and re-typed, dozens of times, all of the text that you will read. Her patience is legendary, and for that I am grateful. Towards the end of my second year with this book, Helen Spears of Trent's Prints in Pace, Florida took over melding photographs with captions and composing the covers and the format of my project. Steve Blair, a local graphic artist, provided the map of our region for the inside covers. My daughter, Kristin, provided several drawings, the saw palmetto at the bottom of this page as well as the drawings of the bald cypress in the section, "To Plant a Tree." I also had three reviewers that helped edit my book as to factual content, and even spelling and punctuation. I am indebted to Dan Mullins, Teresa Friday and Mike Wiggins who got me through to the final manuscript.

One final thank you goes to Ellie who graces the Crape Myrtle on page 61. Her enchanting smile tells me that she loves trees as much as I do.

THE REVIEWERS

Dan Mullins is a native of the northeast corner of Mississippi. He graduated from Mississippi State University with a B.S. and M.S. in ornamental horticulture. In 1970 he began his career as a Horticultural Extension Agent in Escambia County, Florida. In 1977 he relocated back to his home town in Mississippi. There he started and ran a landscape and design business for the next 12 years. In 1989, Dan returned to the Gulf Coast as a Santa Rosa County Horticultural Extension Agent. The agents are now part of the faculty of the University of Florida's Institute of Food and Agricultural Science. As one of Florida's longest serving Extension Agents, now 27 years, he has written extensively for the local media, as well as for university publications.

Teresa Friday was born in Selma, Alabama, but as a self-described "Air Force brat" she grew up living in many parts of this country, as well as abroad. Her career began as a medical technologist in Pensacola, Florida, but her interest lay elsewhere. She received her B.S. degree in Environmental Horticulture, and her Master Degree in Agriculture, both from the University of Florida. Since 2001, Teresa has been working as an Extension Agent in Santa Rosa County, Florida. Her interest in native plants and environmentally friendly landscapes is evident from the weekly columns she writes for the Pensacola News Journal.

Mike Wiggins is a native, and life long resident of the Gulf Coast. His father opened Escambia Farmer's Supply in Pensacola, Florida in the 1940s, so when Mike was old enough he became involved in the agricultural and horticultural retail trade at the family owned business. He continued to run the store until he sold the business in 1995. Mike received a B.S. degree in finance from Florida State University, and has additional horticultural course work from Pensacola Junior College. He has been a local presence on television for 25 years, hosting his own show on Gulf Coast plants and their care. Mike is also a Florida certified pest control operator, and currently owns Wiggins Lawn Spray Service for lawns and ornamental landscapes. In 2008 Mike was honored to be elected by the residents of the city of Pensacola to serve as their mayor.

INTRODUCTION

Like the majority of Gulf Coast residents, I am a transplant. I moved here in 1983 from Ft. Lauderdale, Florida where I ran a proprietary psychiatric hospital. Prior to that, I ran a small public psychiatric hospital in North Carolina, which is my home state. My career move to the Gulf Coast was as administrator of an alcohol and drug abuse facility. My formal education, from the University of North Carolina, is in economics and health care administration, *not* horticulture. So it was through a great deal of trial and perhaps more error that I bought my first home in Gulf Breeze, Florida and began landscaping it. On my much appreciated weekends, when I didn't have to wear a coat and tie, I would search out plants, sod and trees from local nurseries.

I remember successes, like planting a small 'Professor Sargent' *Camellia japonica* in the right spot in my front yard, but I also remember some memorable false starts and errors such as lining my new pool deck with loquat trees. I didn't know at that time that my dozen or so loquats would virtually rain leaves and fruit into the pool and create more work than enjoyment.

Five years after moving to Gulf Breeze my health care company reorganized and sold my alcohol and drug abuse facility. Like many displaced midlevel executives, I held myself out as a health care consultant for two years before realizing that I would not be able to feed my family much longer without working full time. I had job offers in different parts of the country, but I was spoiled by the laid back lifestyle and reasonably cooperative weather of the Gulf Coast.

I decided to follow my heart, but not necessarily my schooling in economics. I bought two acres of land and opened a lawn and garden center. Since 1989 I have owned and operated Mike's Garden in Gulf Breeze, Florida. While I never did attain any formal training in horticulture, I became, out of economic necessity, an astute observer of landscape design and landscape plants for the Gulf Coast.

The Gulf Coast, from New Orleans, Louisiana to Apalachicola, Florida, is a unique environment for plants. Over this 400 mile linear geography, we share hardiness zones, heat zones, inches of annual rain, humidity, sand and soils, salt air and an unfortunate propensity for huge wind events (think Camille, Ivan, Katrina and dozens of others.)

Through this book I hope to give new as well as long time homeowners on the Gulf Coast a guide on where to begin and how to succeed in landscaping your home. It is a guide, if you will, for the beginner who is not even sure of the right questions to ask. I was there! I feel your pain! This book is for you!

Mike Robertson

THE CLIMATE

I have chosen to limit the scope of this book to the coastal counties and parishes between New Orleans, Louisiana and Apalachicola, Florida. There are two reasons for the limitation:

1) Shared climate
2) I know what works here

Many of the same tips might be germane to the coastal counties between St. Augustine, Florida and Charleston, South Carolina, and other similar areas in other parts of the world, but for this writer my experience and "astute observations" are limited to the upper Gulf Coast.

Temperature

On the website, quickcast.com, you can locate your nearest coastal city and learn what average temperatures you can expect. I did for the major cities and towns along the Gulf Coast.

Temperature in degrees Fahrenheit

	Average Daily High in July	Highest Recorded Any month	Average Daily Low in January	Lowest Recorded Any Month	Precipitation in Inches annually
Apalachicola, FL	89	99	44	9	58
Panama City, FL	88	101	45	11	56
Pensacola, FL	90	106	43	5	63
Mobile, AL	91	104	41	3	66
Biloxi, MS	90	*	42	*	62
New Orleans, LA	91	102	43	11	62

* incomplete data

The statistics above cover from 30 to 48 years, depending on the town, so we can assume the numbers are not flukes. We can now generalize somewhat about our balmy coast. During the summer months of June, July and August we will on average have many days where the temperature will hit 90 degrees. Fortunately, we live near the coast and so our highs are moderated by the sea, so we rarely swelter in temperatures above 100 degrees. In the winter months of December and January it can get cold at night, but freezes are somewhat rare; only an average of 13 freezes per year in New Orleans and 15 freezes in Pensacola.

We get a lot of rain on the Gulf Coast, about 5 feet per year. But it too varies somewhat year to year; 29" to 93" in Pensacola and 39" to 102" in New Orleans. We can also have huge rain events such as 27.62" recorded in 36 hours in Gulf Breeze, Florida in 2007! But keep in mind that it is also not unusual for parts of the Gulf Coast to endure one or two months of drought. In very porous, well drained, sandy soils many plants will succumb without irrigation.

While averages are important, temperature extremes can kill plants that would ordinarily survive. During the late 1980s and early 1990s, we had extremely low temperatures along the Gulf Coast. On one occasion the mercury dipped to 5 degrees Fahrenheit right here in Gulf Breeze, Florida. That one night was enough to kill well established pindo palms, Washington palms, and several cultivars of St. Augustine grass. Another year the temperature dropped to 12 degrees, but went up only to 20 degrees during the day and went back down to 12 degrees that evening. A "hard freeze" is defined as an episode of temperature 26 degrees or colder for 5 or more hours. During these hard freezes, normally safe or cold hardy plants can be damaged or killed; including azaleas, Japanese yew and pittosporum. Averages are important for plants to thrive, but extremes impact their ability to survive. The damage may not become evident until it warms in the spring or summer. Many times I've seen plants with bark that has been split by extreme cold, but not show evidence of decline until later in the year.

Gulf Breeze is located on a 15 mile strip of land that separates the sound, or intracoastal from a large bay 3 to 12 miles wide. Luckily, north wind in the winter is moderated by several degrees. Many times we will hear of temperatures in the 20s in northern Escambia and Santa Rosa Counties, when at the same time we are experiencing lows in the 30s. Micro climates are very important to plants. Not only do temperatures vary widely within a few miles, but will also vary around your home. Note that colder air sinks to lower spots in your neighborhood. While someone's sago survives at the top of the hill, another may succumb to a freeze at the bottom.

Most freezes occur at night on the Gulf Coast, so the sun rising in the east and first warming eastern and southern exposures is a welcome relief. Always consider these exposures first for the installation of less "hardy" plants. By the way, the word "hardy" in the horticultural sense <u>only</u> refers to <u>cold</u> hardiness, nothing more. To find out about a plant's overall toughness, always ask your nurseryman specific questions regarding sun tolerance, wind tolerance or drought tolerance. Will it take moist conditions? If you simply ask if the plant is hardy, he or she may answer yes. You may then install the plant in a sunny spot and have it die within weeks because it was a shade lover. Planting next to a swimming pool can raise a plant's survivability. Also, courtyard situations or even an architectural alcove can make a big difference in a plant's survivability. Both of these situations reduce the desiccating effects of the north wind, as well as help to capture and hold heat.

USDA Plant Hardiness Zones

The United States Department of Agriculture has conveniently divided our country into 11 plant hardiness zones; starting with zone 1 for coldest to zone 11 for warmest. The eleven zones are further divided into a & b ("a" coldest, "b" warmest).

Living in zone 1 means that your <u>average *coldest temperature*</u> is minus 50 degrees Fahrenheit or less (such as in Fairbanks, Alaska). Living in zone 11 means your average coldest temperature will be above 40 degrees Fahrenheit (such as Key West, Florida).

This measure is more useful than the average low for any one month or year. This measure is one which tells you that over the course of several years you can expect the temperature to drop this low.

The Gulf Coast counties between Apalachicola and New Orleans are in the zones 8a, 8b, and 9a. Those lowest temperatures you expect over several years are 10° - 15° in 8a, 15°- 20°in 8b, or 20° - 25° in 9a. Keep in mind that the zone designations are inexact. In fact, the draft of a new map has been produced and should be out shortly. It is of course, based on more recent temperature recordings. The maps are based on major weather reporting stations. For example, I know that 9a more closely reflects the Gulf Breeze climate, but on the map Gulf Breeze is currently listed as 8b. The new map reportedly shows the Gulf Coast roughly divided by Interstate 10. North of Interstate 10 is zone 8, while south of Interstate 10 is zone 9. I think this is a much more accurate representation of my town of Gulf Breeze. Try to interpret, if you will, your own yard and micro climate to assign it a zone.

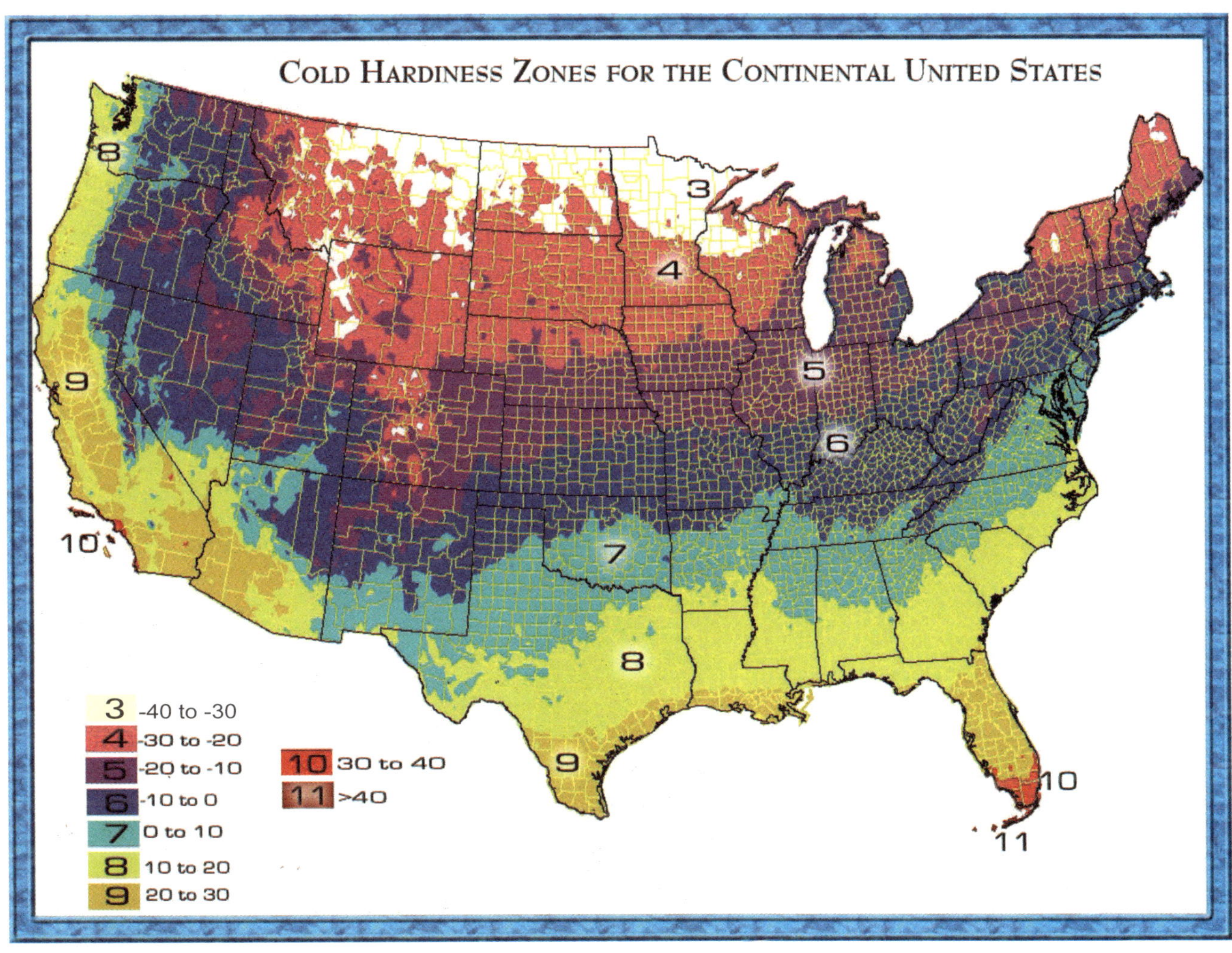

One reason these zones are important to understand is that most books which list and describe plants will include a zone reference. So when reading the reference you will know that placing that pygmy date palm in zones 8 or 9 is a risk. But what about planting it in an alcove, facing south, beside a swimming pool? Possibly!

What do you do when extreme cold is headed your way? Cold that drops temperatures below the averages and near records.

1) Know which plants are cold hardy. Concentrate on protecting the others.
2) Thoroughly water the half-hardy, or more tropical plants 24 hours before the freeze arrives. A well watered plant is much more likely to survive.
3) Bring potted plants indoors, or at least inside an unheated garage. Even having plants under an overhang offers some protection.
4) You can cover your plants. Cover the entire plant with a cloth sheet or blanket and anchor the wrap to the ground to capture some ground heat. Plastic does not work as well, and where the plastic is in contact with the leaves or fronds, cold burn may occur. If you desire, you can build a cold frame using plastic sheeting. The structure becomes a miniature green house for the plant. I have seen people use lights to heat the cold frame, which would be more effective.

Personally, I have never covered my plants. Perhaps I'm too lazy. If I lose a plant in a certain spot, I begin anew with a more cold hardy plant. And I do have some rather cold tender plants in my yard (citrus, queen palms, and even tibouchina), but their location in my yard is particularly chosen for a slightly warmer microclimate.

5) Turn off and drain your sprinkler pump if a hard freeze is predicted. Pumps can be expensive to replace.

After the freeze:

1) Uncover your plants (heat buildup in a cold frame can kill the plant as well)
2) Re-prime your sprinkler pump and turn it back on
3) Re-water your plants

Night-blooming Cereus that is planted just outside my back door. In the cactus family, this half-hardy plant blooms 3 or 4 times during the summer. Its blooms only begin to open after dark and begin to shrivel and die at mornings first light. But for a short time on some of the warmest nights of the year, this plant has some of the most spectacular blooms in the plant kingdom. Virtually every winter I lose a large part of the plant to cold but it recovers in the summer.

A.H.S. Heat Zones

Heat stress is another factor when considering the selection of plants for your yard. To gain insight into their susceptibility along the Gulf Coast you might consult the American Horticultural Society's Heat Zone Map. This map was only first published in 1997. While not nearly as referenced as cold hardiness zones, it is quite useful in screening out plants for the Gulf Coast.

Most new homeowners in our area want to bring some remembrance of their former, more northern home. But the plants may not make it here due to the heat stress of our summers. Some common requests we get at the nursery are for lilacs, forsythia, mountain laurel, Douglas firs and cherry trees; none of which do well here. Hundreds of other plants also do not do well in our heat zones, but do quite well in more northern climates.

These plants are sometimes sold here, so, buyers beware! The stress of our continually warm (make that hot) summer days do not kill the plant over night, but allow the suffering plant to linger for months or even several years before capitulating to the inevitable.

This heat zone map divides the U.S. into 12 zones which average 86°Fahrenheit, or above, for a certain number of days per year. We along the Gulf Coast are living in heat zones 8 & 9. Zone 8 is right along the Coast and projects 90 to 120 days where highs meet or exceed 86°. Further inland where the sea breezes may not reach, the heat zone is designated a 9, which projects 120 to 150 days of 86°and above.

Chill Hours

One more weather related category to learn and you qualify for the Gulf Coast horticultural climate merit badge – Chill Hours. This is another important reference to understand when selecting plants, particularly those plants that require dormancy to produce flowers or fruit in warmer months. For example, the Gulf Coast may never be able to commercially produce as many varieties of apples, pears, or peaches as North Carolina, Washington State or Georgia. It is not because of extreme cold or even the hot months of summer. It is rather because most of these flowering and fruiting trees require a lengthy dormancy that our climate may not be able to sustain with continuously cool temperatures.

A chill hour is basically one hour of time at 45° Fahrenheit or below. When choosing deciduous, flowering trees, e.g., crabapple or cherry, or deciduous fruiting trees, e.g., apple, pear, peach or plum, it is of vital importance to know how many chill hours they require. Our Gulf Coast averages about 350 to 450 chill hours each year in the southern portions of our counties. The northern parts of our counties average 450 to 700 chill hours per year. Luckily for us, several of the above mentioned fruit trees can be obtained in "low chill hour" varieties. While higher chill hour varieties may be found and purchased, you will surely be disappointed in their lack of fruit.

The only other thing I will mention in this chapter that makes us unique in terms of climate is moisture. We have high humidity levels. The continuous moisture level in the air can contribute to mold or fungus on plants. This will be a concern if you are moving from a dryer but otherwise similar climate. Many transplanted Californians want fuchsia baskets like they had back home. Unfortunately our humidity will contribute to the fuchsia's quick demise. We also have to choose figs that have a "closed eye" such as "Brown Turkey" and "Celeste", rather than the large "open eye" varieties that California can produce.

Extreme cold, hot summers, high humidity, few cold nights, rain measured in feet, and wind events referenced in history books - welcome to the Gulf Coast! This environment may seem hostile to plants, but in reality commercial Gulf Coast nurseries produce and ship millions of plants to the rest of the country. You think nothing will grow here – just leave a cleared Gulf Coast building lot bare. At year's end you will have a collection of several species of native trees, several types of grasses, and several dozen assorted vines, shrubs and other weeds. In short, this is a hospitable and even terrific place for literally thousands of landscape plant varieties. You may not be able to select that particular favorite plant from your former home, but I can show you several alternatives that will meet or exceed your expectations.

THE SOILS

Most, if not all, new homeowners to our area are astonished at our soil, or as they think, the lack of it. Close to the coast the soil is mostly sand, and in some areas it is virtually 100% clean, white sand. In other low wetland areas, the soil may be a solid black, loamy soil. In still other areas of higher elevation, the soil may have a clay component. The three main components of soil are sand, silt and clay. We have all three along the Gulf Coast, but by far the most prevalent is the very sandy version.

When I first went into business in 1989, we sold peat moss and cow manure or mushroom compost with virtually every plant to "amend" or augment the existing soil. It was thought a necessity for the proper installation of any plant. In the early 1990s, the University of Florida, issued new guidelines to our County Extension offices. These new guidelines were repeated in agricultural institutes across the country. Amending the soil to install a plant is unnecessary. Not only did studies show it to be unnecessary to amend the soil, but in many instances the inclusion of amendments into the native soil actually caused the roots of the plant to remain only in the amended soil. For a tree or plant that needs expansive root structure for stability in wind, and sufficient root structure to survive droughts this could be a significant handicap.

I give the same advice today, "No amendments in isolated plantings." Amendments are still fine for potted plants in single pots or large planters, of course. Also, amendments are particularly important in vegetable gardens. A raised bed with plenty of organic amendments is much better for your garden for at least two reasons: 1) the exchange of water and nutrients in a loamy organic mix is much better than in our course sand, and

2) nematodes, which can be plant root parasites, move much more slowly in organic materials and will inflict less damage on the plants than in sandy soils.

The only other place I advise people to amend is in bedded areas where a variety of landscape plants are to be used. This is especially true if the home or building is newly constructed. New construction involving concrete block, brick or stucco all include heavy doses of mortar and lime which have leached or been dumped into the soil. Driveways, sidewalks and curbs of concrete also tend to lime the soil and thus raise the pH or alkalinity of our soils. Our native soils are usually in the 5.0 to 8.0 range. The 8.0 end of the range would be found on the barrier islands where years of shell accumulation has naturally raised the pH in the sand. The lower end of the scale is going to be found further inland where the accumulation of organic debris has made the soils more acid. Amending a bed means putting things like aged pine bark (finely ground), sphagnum peat, and animal manures on top of the entire area to be bedded, and tilling in the mixture to a depth of 6" to 8". A shovel will work for this, but a small tiller is much faster and does a much better job. Once the bed is thoroughly tilled, you will notice that you have actually lofted the bed several inches. Now with a rake, always slope the bed away from the building so that water will drain away. When planting the plants, some amendments will naturally be introduced around the root ball, but that's okay, the plant's entire root environment is amended soil.

A number of our customers worry about needing to lime their soil to make it more neutral, or closer to a pH of 7. Again, most of the plants that do well here tolerate our acid soils. I never advise someone to lime the soil unless the soil is tested for the suitability of a particular crop or plant. Indiscriminate liming rarely pans out. However, when lime is recommended, it is usually dolomitic lime (sometimes called dolomite). It contains substantial amounts of calcium and magnesium which are important plant nutrients. Homeowners will want to purchase pelletized dolomite, which is not as messy as the powdered version.

Acidifiers are sometimes used, particularly for acid loving plants such as azaleas, gardenias, camellias or blueberries. If your soil needs to be made more acidic, consider amending with finely shredded pine bark and mulching with pine bark nuggets or pine straw. Soil acidifiers such as wettable sulfur or aluminum sulfate will lower pH for a short period of time (perhaps a season), but the effects will be lost in the long run.

To sum up and advise on this rather complex and tedious subject of pH, "Go with what you've got." Most plants are tolerant of a fairly wide range of pH, so if certain types of plants are failing in your soil because of pH, change the plants.

EQUIPMENT AND TOOLS

If you own a home with the typical suburban lot of a quarter acre, there are tools and equipment that you will need to improve or maintain your landscape. For your lawn, of course, you may want to hire a lawn maintenance guy that mows, edges, weed eats and blows clean the walks and drives. I have such a service. It costs me each time he comes, but I don't have the expense and hassle of owning a mower, edger, line trimmer and blower. I don't have to buy and store gasoline, and I have extra space in my garage where the machines would be kept. And last, but not least, my free time is more free than my neighbors who mow their lawns themselves. But not everyone has a lawn maintenance service, so here are a few tips for buying the equipment.

"Zero Turn Radius" Mower. Very efficient but the most expensive of mower options. Prices have fallen in recent years however.

The mower: Buy a good quality 6 H.P. and above, 4-cycle mulching mower. Rarely should you ever need to bag clippings. A mower with over sized rear wheels is easier to maneuver. A self propelled option is something you might want to consider. Expect to pay $300 to $500. If you are considering an inexpensive riding mower – don't! They are a chore to maintain, slow and disappointing. The next step up that you should consider is a zero turn radius mower. They are easy to operate and will cut your mowing time dramatically. It is a big toy for big boys. Expect to pay $3,000 and up.

The edger and line trimmer: Buy a combination 2 cycle edger and line trimmer. They make very good combinations now, and in fact the edger in a combination is really lighter and easier to use than the older three wheel models with their own four cycle engines. You can also add additional components to your combination unit, such as a hedge trimmer or tiller. Expect to pay $300 and up for the combination.

String Trimmer. This particular model accepts several different attachments.

The blower: I really hate blowers because of the excessive noise they make, but they do save many sweep strokes of a quiet unassuming broom. Buy a 2 cycle, lightweight, hand held blower. Expect to pay $100 plus for a good one.

To maintain your lawn, you need all of the above. If you feel you can get by with just a mower, please go ahead and hire the yard service. Your neighbors will appreciate it.

Hand tools must also be stocked in your garage to maintain your landscape. Even if you have a yard service, you will find that they are reluctant to use anything without an engine. Thus the expression, "They mow, edge, blow and go."

Periodically you will have the need for these hand tools and equipment:

1) long handle round point shovel
2) long handle flat head shovel
3) garden rake
4) leaf rake
5) wheel barrow or garden cart
6) pruners
7) loppers
8) shears
9) pruning saw
10) sprayer (pump)
11) spreader (broadcast)

For the average homeowner, hand tools can last a lifetime, so buy the best ones available at your hardware, garden center, or home improvement store. My favorite round point shovel is one that has a steel handle. It is heavier than most, which allows the inertia of the shovel to power through roots and hard soils. For women, or lighter individuals, they also make good shovels with handles of wood or fiberglass. Never, however, buy a short handled shovel. I cannot for the life of me even fathom what the purpose of such a shovel is, unless you were very short – say under four feet. No, even then, a long handle shovel is better.

Why do you need both a round point shovel and a flat head shovel? It's quite simple. A round point you will use 90% of the time to dig holes, dig up plants for transplanting, fill a wheel barrow, etc. The second type of shovel, the flathead, is useful for cleaning debris off of pavement or flat ground. It will be used only 10% of the time, but it will be sorely missed when you do need it.

Left to right - Round Point and Flat Head Shovels

The two rakes that are a must for a homeowner are a garden rake and a leaf rake. A garden rake (or bow rake) has stiff, steel tines and is useful for leveling or grading soil, amending soil, raking mixed heavy debris, etc. The leaf rake is useful for raking leaves (duh!), plus pine straw, clippings and light debris. It is also useful for giving parts of your lawn a hard raking to help remove remaining thatch and even some broadleaf weeds in early spring. And nothing is better to give loose soil a final finished grade. I would recommend that you stay away from the plastic tine varieties and stick with the flexible metal tines for a better, more efficient rake.

Left to right - Leaf Rake and Garden Rake leaning against a heavy duty wheelbarrow.

Another piece of equipment that should be in your garage is something to move landscape materials from place to place. I personally prefer a wheel barrow. One can move a very heavy load with a construction grade wheel barrow. A good, heavy duty one will cost about $100. I prefer the metal to the plastic tub because I have seen the plastic ones warp and even break under load. Something quite worthwhile when purchasing a wheel barrow would be consideration of a solid rubber wheel barrow tire. This is not the old fashion hard rubber tire, but a firm foam tire that rolls and gives when necessary, like an inflatable tire. Inflatable wheel barrow tires are easily subject to puncture or slow leaks. When you have to inflate or repair your tire on a regular basis, you will wish you had one of the new solid tires in spite of their being rather pricey. Of course I'm recommending a heavy duty wheel barrow that will haul 6 cu.ft. It's easy for me to move around, but I'm 6'1" tall and weigh 200 pounds. For most women, or individuals of slighter build, a two wheel utility cart might serve well. I think that would be more useful than a light weight wheel barrow.

Pruning trees and shrubs is one of my favorite things to do. If done correctly, at the right time and with the right tool, it's good for your heart, your soul and good for the plant. You may think you only need one tool to prune correctly, but you need all four as listed above. For cuts up to about ½", a pair of pruners is best. I really hate to tell you this, but a fairly accurate guide to the quality of a tool is its price! Again, a quality tool can last a lifetime of homeowner use. Look for a major brand of bypass pruners which use a scissor action and expect to pay $30 plus for a good pair. If arthritis is a problem, you might consider a pair of ratcheting pruners. They are much easier to squeeze and are very light weight.

A pair of two handed loppers is another tool you will want in your arsenal. A good set of loppers can easily handle branches of 1" to 1 ½" in diameter. Expect to pay $35. plus. You can buy larger professional, compound loppers that will make cuts of 2" and up, but for homeowner use they are probably superfluous. That is because a well armed homeowner will also have a pruning saw. A high quality pruning saw will quickly take those branches of 2" to 4". Expect to pay about $40 for a good one.

Left to right - Pruners, Loppers, Pruning Saw. Three must have tools.

The last "must have" to prune is a pair of hedge shears. This tool has long handles for leverage and long blades for cutting many small terminal branches at once. This type of pruning is called "shearing" where you shape and/or reduce the size of a shrub like an azalea or boxwood. Again, a good quality one will sell for about $50.

Other tools you might want to consider include a chainsaw, a pole pruner and pruning scissors. A chainsaw is invaluable if you have trees come down on your property after a hurricane. However, most homeowners will use it too infrequently to become proficient in its use. For that reason, I don't recommend that every homeowner go out and buy one. They can remove limbs from the user as quickly as limbs from trees. The average homeowner is much better served to hire a licensed, qualified tree service for those rare occasions when a chainsaw is necessary.

Many homeowners have a pole pruner for, again, the rather infrequent times you need to remove small tree branches out of your reach. Having one will reduce your need to use a ladder to reach those branches. I have a high quality one, but I still find it cumbersome, unwieldy and unable to provide quality cuts exactly where I want them, but I still use it to prune occasionally. Pruning scissors can be purchased for less than $15. and can be useful for finer cuts on roses or herbaceous perennials.

A couple of other pieces of equipment will be needed to care for your lawn and shrubs. Several times per year you will need a broadcast spreader. This is a walk behind push cart that spreads fertilizer, grass seed, herbicides, fungicides or insecticides in granular form. The spread of the thrower is about 4' to 8', depending on the spreader and speed with which you walk. Another type of spreader available is a drop spreader, which evenly drops the material under the machine as you walk. A drop spreader has its place, but it is not in your garage, a broadcast spreader is much more useful for the homeowner. A better one will have larger wheels, a wider stance and a larger hopper. You should be able to get by for about \$50 to \$75. They vary greatly in price according to the materials they are constructed of; plastic vs. steel vs. stainless steal, hard plastic wheels vs. inflatable tires. Just a fairly basic one will do.

A pump up tank sprayer is another piece of equipment I strongly recommend to maintain your landscape. You can buy a good 1 ½ gallon plastic tank with a brass wand for about \$30 to \$40. Chemicals you buy to combat diseases or infestations on your grass or landscape plants may come in a ready to use, 24 oz. spray bottle, but most of the pesticides, herbicides or fungicides also come in concentrates that will make gallons of product for less money. A pump up sprayer is easy to use, easy to mix the chemicals in, and does a great job of atomizing the spray so as to thoroughly coat the leaves of the plant. I rarely recommend a hose end sprayer for those same reasons. A hose end sprayer can be complicated to calibrate and mix appropriately, and the spray comes out in larger droplets which are not as effective at coating the plant.

If you are a tool aficionado like me, you might acquire other more specialized tools, but the ones I have listed above are ones you must have and be able to use to maintain your landscape.

Left to right - Trigger Spray Bottle, Pump Sprayer, Hose End Sprayer

A word about spray and fertilizing services; I do not ordinarily recommend that homeowners contract with one. It is much more cost effective to establish a good relationship with your local garden center or County Extension Service to get information on appropriate treatment and fertilization of your landscape. A typical suburban home should require an expenditure of less than \$200 per year for chemicals and fertilizers to keep the lawn, trees and shrubs in tip top shape. However, if you have little time or interest in the routine maintenance of your lawn, a licensed spray service may be just what you need.

THE SPRINKLER SYSTEM

I wish I could tell you that a sprinkler system is not necessary for a Gulf Coast home. Unfortunately because of our consistently hot summers, very sandy soils and regular droughts, you will most likely need a sprinkler system.

First the Exceptions

1) If you have no lawn and you just have bedded areas, you can establish new plantings with hose watering. Frequent applications for a few weeks should be followed by less and less frequency.

2) If your home is located in an area with a very high water table you may not need a sprinkler system. For example, at my home if I dig down 2' or more in my yard, water begins seeping in and filling the bottom of the hole. That's a high water table. The water table does fluctuate though, and occasionally during summer droughts I am forced to drag hoses and sprinkle parts of my yard. Other times the roots of my grass, shrubs and trees are reaching into the water table for a drink.

However, most of you will not have a high water table, and you will need a sprinkler system to water your lawn. I have watched many homeowners try to get by without one, and religiously try to keep up a watering schedule with hoses. Then comes summer. Then comes a six week drought (which is not uncommon). Then comes time for the homeowner's vacation when the family leaves for just a week or two, and returns home to find they have lost thousands of dollars worth of lawn. Do not put in a lawn until your sprinkler system is in place, and working!

There is no sprinkler system to water my grass or plants yet part of my backyard resembles a jungle (to screen the hot tub). My property backs up to a wetland so my yard has a high water table.

I, for one, do not think installing a sprinkler system is a "do it yourself" job for the average homeowner, but many homeowners try, and a few even succeed. I am not sure of all of the state's laws on this subject, but in Florida:

1) A permit is required from the Water Management District to put in a well.

2) Testing and state licensure is required to professionally install sprinkler systems. Flow rates, water pressure, correct use of sprinkler heads, compatibility of pump to system are all important considerations.

3) A licensed electrician is required for final hook up of the electrical components.

All of the above, plus the toil of trenching work make it a job for professionals. A few guidelines may help.

You can opt for an initially less expensive option. Save on the well and pump, and just have your system hooked to the tap or city water. But you will most likely find that your water bill is somewhere between very high and astronomical. Rarely is the use of city water on an ongoing basis a viable option.

A source of landscape water that is coming into greater use is that of "grey water", or reuse water. Grey water is waste water that has been treated to the point of removing all solids, and purified to the point of making it safe for public exposure. It is being sold by municipalities very cheaply, or even provided for free. It is a terrific ecologically beneficial alternative to tapping into our ground water, and saves you the cost of a well and pump.

The first task then is the well. Fortunately for some of the Gulf Coast, a 2" diameter well can be "hand bailed" to a depth of about 30'. The well at my nursery is only 17'. Others produce sufficient water at less than 12'. Unfortunately many on the Gulf Coast will find that their elevation is too high and/or their soils cannot be "hand bailed." In those instances, your sprinkler contractor will have to bring in a well drilling machine (usually a separate contractor) to drill a well. A successful irrigation well is one that can produce 40 gallons per minute. The water should be free of excessive salt, and low in iron, sulfur or other pernicious elements. If salt or an excess of other elements are present in a shallow well, a deeper one needs to be drilled. A reminder - the water from your sprinkler well is not potable (not drinkable). Remind your kids! The pumps used for shallow well homeowner systems are generally 1 ½ H.P. that run on a 220 volt connection. Deeper wells may require a larger pump, of course. Your unit will have a drain plug in the bottom for freeze preparation, and a large plug or hose bib (faucet) at the top for refilling the pump after the freeze.

Reminder – If the forecast for your area is freezing, you should drain your pump to keep it from cracking. To do this, take out the drain plug and open the plug on top, or "turn on" the hose bib at the top. Don't forget to turn the system off so that the pump will not run unprimed. When the freeze is over, you have to prime, or fill it with water. Factoid – these pumps will not pump air, so they can't suck the water from the well without having water in the pump to begin with.

Near the pump may be an above ground P.V.C. contraption that allows the system to mechanically switch zones (or areas to be watered). Most homeowner systems will accommodate four to six zones. Be sure that your bedded areas are on separate zones from the grassed areas because established landscape plants will require less water than your established lawn. Zones can also be switched electronically in more elaborate systems. This gives you more flexibility in choosing what zone to water when.

Another very important component to the system is the timer. Some are largely mechanical with rotating dials and pins to start and stop cycles. Many of the newer timers are computerized. One of my pet peeves is a timer that may be easy to program for the installer, but nevertheless is as simple as a Rubik cube for the owner. You will need to change the program on your timer to adjust for seasons, rain events and droughts. Don't be stuck with a timer that you can't easily program, or have to refer to a lengthy set of instructions to reset. On many occasions I have been asked to explain and adjust sprinkler timers for homeowners. Many I can adjust, but some remind me of programming to record a favorite show on one of the early VHS recorders! If your installer brings you a timer that you cannot readily understand and adjust, send it back! You owe him no excuses. You owe your landscape a chance to thrive and make your home beautiful.

Many different types of sprinkler heads are on the market today. Three basic types of heads are:

1) Rotational – for grassed areas. These will rotate in areas from 15 degrees to 360 degrees. Some pop up out of the grass and some are on risers. You don't want rotational heads in bedded areas.

2) Spray heads – for bedded areas, are available in different spray patterns to efficiently cover irregular bedded areas. Some are on risers; some pop up out of the ground when activated.

3) Bubblers – for large specimen plants that need large amounts of water delivered right over the root ball. These are easily adjustable as the plant grows and needs less irrigation.

A few guidelines:

You should have overlapping coverage of your sprinklers, i.e. if a rotational head will spray a distance of 30', have another head placed 30' from that one to give you 200% coverage. When your system is working perfectly you only have to use it one half the time of a system set up for 100% coverage. Also, if a head is clogged or broken, the plants will still get water.

Be sure your heads do not put water on your building, drives, walks, etc. Most all wells will pump water that has some discoloration to it. It's only a matter of time until the spray patterns are etched indelibly onto your hardscape.

Make sure your heads are placed on a generous amount of "funny pipe", or flexible tubing that is in turn attached to inflexible P.V.C. pipe. This allows you to easily move heads 18" or so. You will periodically need to do this as your shrubs grow, or other plants are installed or removed.

After your system is installed, be sure all of your plants are getting adequate coverage. If you add beds or reconfigure bedded areas, don't hesitate to call back your sprinkler installer to add or adjust heads. They should easily be able to install extra lines and heads into an existing bedded area without disturbing the plants.

Infrequently some sprinkler systems with shallow wells along our coast begin pumping salt water. These periods of salt water intrusion into the water table usually follow periods of drought. If you begin to see several varieties of your landscape plants browning at the edges and tips of their leaves, you may have a problem. Collect a sample of your well water, and then turn your system off until you have your sample tested and it is clear of salt. The only thing worse for most plants than no water is salt water. If salt water intrusion becomes a recurring nuisance, you will want to have your well deepened or relocated.

THE LAWN BASICS

Your lawn is probably the most costly of landscape investments. A typical one third acre subdivision lot may have 5,000 to 10,000 square feet of house, drive, walks and bedded area, so the remainder is usually grass. Ten thousand square feet of sod laid down on a prepared yard is expensive. Properly maintained lawns can last a lifetime, but poorly maintained ones can die in a few weeks. Repeating that initial investment is not something most of us ever want to do.

Choosing the Grass

There are six or so species of grass that are suitable for our region as lawn grasses, however 95% of the lawns in our area are centipede or St. Augustine. While they both can have their negatives, either one makes an excellent Gulf Coast lawn. Therefore, this chapter will pertain to the basics of maintaining relatively low maintenance centipede or St. Augustine.

Being in the lawn and garden business, every month or so I will hear a frustrated homeowner swear he is ready to switch over to centipede from St. Augustine. Then another will come in ready to dig up his entire centipede lawn for St. Augustine. If you have an established lawn, stick with it. Lawns in the worst of shape can be improved and renewed. If you have built a new house and are ready to choose a grass, consider these points:

Cost

Centipede sod costs about a third less than St. Augustine. Centipede can also be seeded, which will cost you much less than sod. A five pound package of Centipede seed will cover 10,000 to 20,000 square feet, and is relatively inexpensive. Plugs of either Centipede or St. Augustine are available and do not differ in cost.

St. Augustine is only available in plugs and sod. A few years ago one company claimed to have developed a seed for St. Augustine, but it has not, for whatever reason, become commercially available on a large scale.

Adaptability

St. Augustine is much more salt tolerant than centipede. If you live on a barrier island or next to a sound or salty bay, your choice should be St. Augustine. St. Augustine is also more shade tolerant than centipede. Under very heavy shade (complete shade under live oaks for example), neither grass will flourish. In moderate shade, St. Augustine will grow very well. In light shade, perhaps under widely spaced pines, either grass is appropriate.

Pests and Disease

Mole crickets can damage centipede to a great degree. Chinch bugs can devastate a St. Augustine lawn. Fungus can attack both, and caterpillars can gorge themselves on a salad of either. In other words, don't choose because of pests and disease. My experience has shown that either can succumb in the worst of circumstances.

Fertilization, Watering and Mowing

Centipede has a slight advantage in these areas. St. Augustine needs to be fertilized once more per year. Centipede can be watered somewhat less, and St. Augustine being the faster grower may need more frequent mowing during the summer months.

Centipede Lawn planted in full sun.

You've Chosen!

No matter your choice, you may sod for an instant lawn. This can be done at any time of the year along the Gulf Coast. You can also plug. Plugs of centipede or St. Augustine are sold in trays of eighteen 4" plugs. If you put these plugs in on about 6" to one foot centers, you should have complete coverage after one growing season. If you are plugging in a large area, rent or buy a "plugger". With one of these very simple hand tools, two persons (one with the plugger to remove the plug of soil, and one to stuff the grass plug) can plant 18 plugs in about 5 minutes.

You can also seed centipede, as I mentioned before. The seed appears very expensive because it is so small, but it goes a very long way for little money.

Centipede grass is not available in varieties, or "cultivars", so once you choose centipede you're done. The same is not true with St. Augustine, which is a hybridized grass available in at least nine different cultivated varieties. All of these cultivated varieties, or cultivars, have particular advantages, but none is perfect.

The Seville cultivar is a semi-dwarf that doesn't need frequent mowing, but in the late 1980s record low temperatures caused a number of disappointed homeowners to lose their entire lawn to hard freezes. The cultivar, Floratam, was developed to be chinch bug resistant, which is a huge advantage, but in recent years the chinch bugs have refined their palettes to such an extent that they will occasionally dine on a fine strand of this resistant variety. Floratam also will not stand up to some of our infrequent cold snaps.

The Raleigh cultivar was developed at North Carolina State University specifically to withstand cold. However, it is not chinch bug resistant (See, I told you there wasn't a perfect variety!), but Raleigh is what I would choose for our Gulf Coast area because of its cold tolerance. While you can treat for chinch bugs, you cannot do a thing about cold weather forecasts.

The most sturdy of lawns would in fact be a mixture of cultivars of St. Augustine with perhaps some centipede in the driest areas. "Pure" lawns of only one cultivar can succumb quickly if bugs, fungus, cold or drought attacks their weakest feature, but a yard of mixed grasses is less vulnerable to overall devastation. It's sort of a survival of the fittest, and if you have had a lawn on the Gulf Coast you know, "It's a jungle out there!"

My own lawn is a mixture of grasses, including several grasses that would be considered weeds in other yards. But frankly, on average it looks better than many other high maintenance, pure lawns. My message here is, you really shouldn't become concerned if you need to plug in a cultivar that is different from the one with which you started. You need not become unglued if your neighbor's grass begins creeping into your ethnically pure lawn. Different grasses in your lawn may actually strengthen your lawn in the long run.

St. Augustine Grass planted in shade of pines and "Natchez" crape myrtle. The red flowers are from "Autumn Embers" "Encore" azaleas.

A Few Words About Sodding, Plugging or Seeding

When sodding, you want a planting area that is relatively level and free of weeds. Some recommend that you amend the soil with peat, clay etc. My experience has shown that you really don't need to. Properly watered and fertilized sod will flourish nicely on virtually any lightly raked or tilled surface. Have the pallets of sod (50 to 55 square yards per pallet, or 450 to 495 square feet) delivered and placed as close to where they are going to be put down as possible. Don't try to save on the delivery fee. At 2,000 pounds per pallet, it will be the best delivery fee you ever spend.

Putting down sod is not rocket science. All you have to do is place the rectangles, green side up, closely abutting each other. Nature will quickly hide your mistakes through soil accretion and sod growth to help level out low spots. More compulsive readers might want to have several bags of top soil available per pallet to help level and fill gaps. But even the most compulsive need not worry about "rolling" sod afterwards with a large, water-filled metal roller. Although frequently recommended, I have found that rolling a yard is somewhere between superfluous and totally worthless. Thoroughly water your instant lawn as soon as you put it down (about ½" of water should do). Continue to water once per day for about six weeks, and then cut back on the frequency and increase the amount of water as described later. Wait about two weeks before fertilizing. A good formulation would be a winterizer, low in nitrogen and phosphorus and high in potassium.

At three to four weeks check your new sod for roots by lifting a corner of a piece. You should have roots 2" to 4" long. If it is well rooted, you can now mow it. Mowing stimulates its spread. <u>Do not</u> put down any weeding agents in the first year of its growth, and avoid "Weed & Feed" until its second year of growth.

Plugging

Plugs are available in centipede and different cultivars of St. Augustine. Plugging does not give you an instant yard, but you can have a great lawn after one growing season (April through August). Probably the biggest disadvantage to plugging a complete yard is that in the time it takes for the plugs to fill in, a number of weeds can gain a toehold in the vacant spaces. You should not use herbicides on a newly sodded or plugged lawn. To help with the weed problem you can seed the vacant spaces with centipede grass with the hope that the centipede will germinate before the weeds. Follow the same watering instructions for a newly sodded yard.

You have now chosen your grass, installed your yard, and at least one year has passed. One must maintain a Gulf Coast lawn using some very simple cultural practices.

Grass Plugger shown with tray of 18 plugs and individual plug. A tray of plugs can be installed in less than 10 minutes.

Mowing

One of the biggest mistakes that well intentioned homeowners make with their St. Augustine or centipede lawns is mowing height. It seems everyone wants to cut the lawn too short. To adjust your mower, put it on a flat concrete surface and measure from the blade down to the concrete. Adjust your blade to 2" to 3" for centipede, and 3" to 4" for most St. Augustine cultivars (Delmar and Pursley Seville can be mowed at 2"). Remember that those long, lush blades of grass are where the grass manufacturers its food to sustain the entire plant. If cut too short, the plant will slowly decline. Also, sharpen the blade regularly. Your grass will know when it's time. Check the end of the grass blades, and if the ends are torn and ragged rather than cleanly cut, then you need to take the blade off and sharpen it for the next mowing. A ragged edge is not just unsightly; the increased surface of the cut edge is conducive to the development of fungal disease. Save yourself time and frustration by sharpening your blade.

We have sandy soils, so dead, decomposing grass clippings do not usually build up and contribute to a thatch problem here. For that reason, return the nutrient rich clippings to your lawn with a mulching mower. Mulched clippings are only a problem if you are removing more than a third of the blade length in any one mowing. In that instance, you should bag and dispose of the clippings. Bagging may also be necessary to help control the spread of certain diseases, or when severe weed infestations are an issue. Grasses grow at different rates throughout the growing season depending on weather, watering, fertilization. etc. Mowing frequently will not hurt the grass, but be sure to follow the general rule of thumb that no mowing should remove any more than 1/3 the length of the blade. What about mowing in different directions each time? Pure poppycock, in my opinion. This bit of advice comes from those who mow golf greens. So if you don't intend to putt on your lawn, mow in any direction you please.

Watering

Here is another major failing of the average weekend gardener. He or she wants to water their lawn 15 to 30 minutes a day, every day. Wrong! Wrong! Wrong! *Infrequently but deeply* is the mantra I want everyone to begin chanting.

Here is what I mean. Your grass should be watered only when it needs it. Your grass will let you know when blades begin to curl from side to side. You may also notice that on a lawn wanting water, the grass does not readily spring back from footprints. Then is the time to water. "But," you say, "I have a sprinkler system with an automatic timer, and I don't have time to check to see if it needs water." Okay then, here is the rule of thumb, adjust according to rain. If the daily high temperature is 80 degrees or over (generally May through September), you need to water three times per week. For daily high temperatures 60 to 80 degrees (during October, November, March and April), you need to water two times per week. For daily high temperatures of about 60 degrees (during December, January and February), you only need to water one time per week. Two surprises here; first, you should never need to water any more than three times per week, even in the driest of summer months. Also, your grass needs water even in the winter when it's dormant.

Watering *deeply* means putting out a lot of water when you water, which should be ¾" to 1" every time. Check different parts of your yard using shallow cans (such as cat food cans) to see how long it takes to put out 1" of water using a sprinkler system. An inch of water will soak 6" to 12" into the ground, and that's where you want the roots of your grass to grow. Shallow watering encourages shallowly rooted lawns that are more prone to drought stress, opportunistic weeds and even damage by mole crickets. Those critters do most of their damage by tunneling and uprooting shallowly rooted lawns. Deeply rooted lawns rarely sustain mole cricket damage. Also, infrequently watered lawns do not suffer as much disease or fungus damage because fungus thrives on constantly wet blades and stolons. Altogether now: *"Infrequently, but deeply!"* (That's watering – not mowing.)

One other caution, if you have a well and pump, you might want to have your water tested during periods of prolonged drought. As mentioned before, salt water intrusion into ground water can occur along the Gulf Coast, and salt is toxic to grass, shrubs and trees.

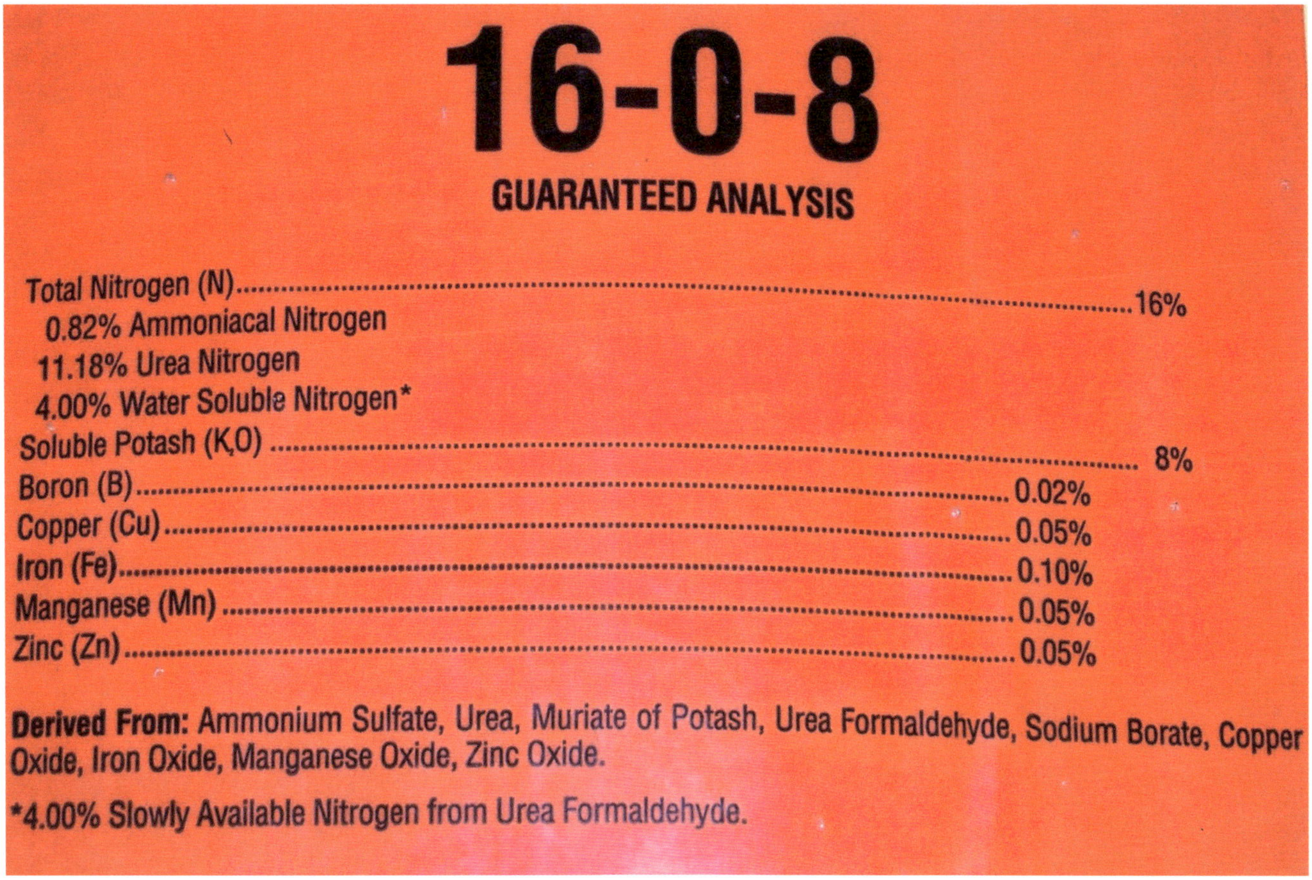

16-0-8

GUARANTEED ANALYSIS

Total Nitrogen (N)	16%
0.82% Ammoniacal Nitrogen	
11.18% Urea Nitrogen	
4.00% Water Soluble Nitrogen*	
Soluble Potash (K_2O)	8%
Boron (B)	0.02%
Copper (Cu)	0.05%
Iron (Fe)	0.10%
Manganese (Mn)	0.05%
Zinc (Zn)	0.05%

Derived From: Ammonium Sulfate, Urea, Muriate of Potash, Urea Formaldehyde, Sodium Borate, Copper Oxide, Iron Oxide, Manganese Oxide, Zinc Oxide.

*4.00% Slowly Available Nitrogen from Urea Formaldehyde.

Fertilizer Analysis shown on every bag of fertilizer. Note the minor elements which are vital in our soils.

Fertilization

You can harm your grass by not giving it enough fertilizer, and you can also harm your grass by fertilizing it too much and too often. Here are some quick, basic rules for fertilization. But first, a short course on lawn fertilizers. You will notice three numbers on any fertilizer bag. These numbers represent, in order, Nitrogen (N) which is necessary for greening and blade growth, Phosphorus (P) for fruiting, flowering, seed production, etc., and Potassium (K). "K"? No wonder so many of us disliked high school chemistry. Potassium is necessary for root production and vigor. You will also notice a list of various micronutrients such as boron, copper, manganese, iron and zinc. These, and a few more trace elements, are all necessary for plant growth.

Applications of fertilizer should be with a high quality, *slow release*, fertilizer. The bags are usually sold to cover an area of 5,000 square feet, so you need to know the square footage of your lawn before shopping for fertilizers. Fertilizers have changed dramatically in the last ten or so years. In my opinion, the old recommendation of a certain number of pounds of nitrogen for every 1,000 square feet, and recommendations of percentages of W.I.N. (water insoluble nitrogen) are confusing and frustrating to the general public. First of all, fertilizers are now blended for a certain time of the year, certain coverage per bag, and even for specific grasses. New fertilizers have time released components with 2, 3 or even 4 month release times. They will advertise their coatings on their basic components, and tell you how long the fertilizer should be active. Others may be urea based formulations which are also slow release. But most importantly, don't try to save money by throwing cheap bags of 8-8-8 on your expensive yard.

The typical 6-6-6, 8-8-8, 10-10-10, etc., fertilizer is an agricultural fertilizer with ammonia based nitrogen useful for perhaps developing a strong stand of corn in a single growing season. If you hope to keep your lawn healthy for more than one season, buy the best complete fertilizers that release slowly and have a good blend of micronutrients in addition to nitrogen, phosphorus and potassium.

What about Weed & Feed? Weed and Feed is a fertilizer with a weeding agent present. It is used primarily in the spring, and may have both pre-emergent and post-emergent qualities. That is, it may kill weed seeds in the ground before they germinate (pre-emergent), or it may kill existing weeds (post-emergent). The chemicals in Weed & Feed that are generally in use are atrazine, simizine, or some other similar sounding names. These chemicals are primarily pre-emergent in action, meaning they will help control the emergence of weeds from seeds. The chemical can last up to 18 months after putting it out. Repeated use every year can build up in your soil, which may not be a good thing. Some of these chemicals are taken up by trees and shrubs, and on some species can have a detrimental effect.

Another chemical that is becoming more widely used in Weed & Feed is trimec, which is a post-emergent product. The instructions for putting this Weed & Feed out include watering the grass prior to spreading it so that it will stick to the blades of the weeds. You then irrigate one to two days later to water the fertilizer into the ground. This post-emergent weed killer and fertilizer can be very effective and it doesn't harm trees and shrubs. While I recommend Weed & Feed, I recommend it only after a lawn has been established for one year, only on a lawn with weed problems, and only to those homeowners that are not going to overseed with annual ryegrass in the fall.

How To Apply

On lawn fertilizers (except those Weed & Feeds with trimec), put the fertilizer out on dry grass blades. A broadcast spreader works best to evenly distribute the fertilizer. Make sure half is put down in one direction, and then spread the other half across that direction for a cross hatched pattern. Otherwise you are almost sure to have streaks of green. While you may be able to set your spreader according to spreader settings on the fertilizer bag, there is no substitute for trial and error. Both your stride and the humidity will affect how much will go out at any rate.

Do not put lime out the same time you put out fertilizer. If you do, the lime can cause the nitrogen to release into the air, and therefore will not do your lawn any good. If you need lime, wait thirty days before fertilizing. If you have already fertilized, wait at least seven days before spreading lime. Once your fertilizer is out, water thoroughly.

For our two most popular Gulf Coast grasses, here are the basics:

St. Augustine: Fertilize to start its growing season, March 1 to April 30. The numbers on the bag may read something like 18-3-4. That gives the grass a lot of nitrogen for blade growth. Our soils need very little phosphorus, and at this time of year the St. Augustine needs little potassium for root growth. Repeat this application 3 months later in June or July.

In October, put out a winterizing fertilizer. It should have a lower first number, a lower middle number and a higher last number. The potassium contributes to root vigor to help the grass during winter.

Centipede: This grass also needs a fertilizer in the spring. Since it is even more sensitive to a buildup of phosphorus in the soil, most good fertilizers specifically blended for centipede will have a 15-0-15 formulation. Phosphorus can actually impede the uptake of nitrogen in centipede. In the summer you should hold off on other "regular" fertilization, but it is useful to put out a winterizer in the fall as it is on St. Augustine. Many times we see centipede get a little off color during the summer. To correct this, try Milorganite (4% Iron), Ironite (4.5% Iron) or one of several chelated liquid iron supplements. This will provide a quick fix to a chlorotic, or yellowish looking color. Micronutrients leach readily in our soils, and may need to be replaced regularly.

Overseeding

You may have noticed that while the majority of lawns on the Gulf Coast seem to brown or go dormant in December, there are others that are greener than ever. This is most likely due to overseeding with an annual ryegrass seed. It can be done at the same time you put out winterizer. The rate of seeding is about 10 pounds per 1,000 square feet, or a 50 pound bag for every 5,000 square feet. The bags are large and heavy, but cheap. Put the seed out in October, November or December. Keep it moist, and within two weeks your lawn will be a lush green again. You never thought you would need to mow on January 1st after heavy partying the night before, but you might. Annual ryegrass grows rapidly and needs regular mowing. Our winters and light freezes won't hurt it, but our hot weather will spell an end to it in about May or June. For all that trouble, annual rye doesn't help your existing lawn, nor does it hurt it, but it will make it look great for the winter. As I mentioned before, avoid weeding agents when using annual ryegrass.

Now you have 95% of what you need to know to establish and keep a very fine lawn on the Gulf Coast. Expenses for fertilizers, pesticides, and a few trays of plugs (to fill in for inevitable small losses) should run less than $200 per year for a 10,000 square foot lawn. For the other 5% of problems, ask your local nurseryman or County Extension Agent. That advice is not only useful, it's free.

LANDSCAPE RULES

In this chapter I want to give you some useful guidelines for landscaping your home, either as a blank palette or as a re-do of an older landscape. Through the years I have developed some rules that I follow to allow for a practical, as well as an aesthetically pleasing effect. My rules will be italicized, and then I will try to explain my rationale.

Simplicity! This cottage style home in Fairhope, Alabama has only 3 varieties of plants in its front bed. They contrast well and do not block the owners' view of the gulf from the porch. The Asiatic jasmine in the foreground is covering a small bank at the street side. Great look!

A landscape design is largely subjective. In other words, you may not want to follow my rules if they do not agree with your idea of aesthetics. As long as this is your last home, and you are not subject to guidelines of a homeowner's association, do what makes you happy.

Design with resale in mind. A tasteful, professionally installed and well maintained landscape will return \$3 + for every \$1 invested upon sale of the home. Sadly, many of our customers are sent to us by real estate agents to give their home some last minute curb appeal before it is listed on the market. Only now with their home up for sale will the owners get to enjoy a more attractive home. Your kitchens and bathrooms may be perfectly updated, but without that inviting landscape, buyers may not ever see the inside of your home. Why not create an appealing, inviting landscape from the start, and enjoy it the whole time you live there?

First things first – after your walk, driveway, patios, etc. are installed at your new home, you need to create bed lines for your home.

Make bed lines curve. Most all homes are rectilinear in design, and part of the purpose of landscaping your home is to soften the lines of the straight walls and 90° corners. Curving the bed lines will help to do that. Many homes in large tract developments end up with straight rows of shrubs planted right up next to the house. That immediately cheapens the house and makes it look smaller than it really is.

Make your beds generous and in scale with the house and lot. Don't skimp on any bed whether it is next to the house, or an island bed away from the house. And besides, the larger your bed, the less grass you have to mow!

Avoid creating mowing difficulties with your bed lines. For example, have your bed extend to the building behind the AC unit, etc. Don't allow small inaccessible patches of grass.

Keep your bed at least 4' wide by your house **because** ***you generally shouldn't plant any closer than 2' from the foundation***. Your beds may undulate from 4' to 12' or more from the foundation, depending on window placement, walks and structural features that you want to complement or screen.

Have a focal point near the front entrance which could be a single specimen plant, a piece of garden sculpture, or a fountain.

Your front entrance should remain the focus so the rest of the landscape should draw the eye to it and compliment it. If your walk comes from the drive and continues to the front door, you should consider bedding the entire area enclosed by the walk, and the entire area opposite the walk heading toward the house. The same is true of circular drives. Consider bedding most, if not all of the area enclosed by the drive. If the walk comes from the street to the front entrance, increase the scope of the landscape as you approach the house.

Next page: These steps to a front entrance are curved and attractive. Because the steps are so generous, there is a lot of red brick for the eye to absorb. These steps were made incredibly interesting with the addition of creeping fig along the face.

Do not block the front entrance with landscaping. The front could be viewed as a funnel from an aerial image with the spout at the front door. The landscaping should remain outside of the funnel. The symbolism remains relevant because you want to entice, or funnel your guests to the front door.

Next, give some thought as to whether you want more of a traditional landscape, a tropical landscape or a combination of each. More and more tropical influence is being seen on our Gulf Coast, even in the yards of very traditional homes. Take a look through your neighborhood, and try for reasonable continuity. You don't want your new, tropically landscaped home to stand out like a drug lord's crib from an episode of Miami Vice.

Once the style of your landscape is chosen and the beds are outlined, it is time to ***pick the trees before you choose the other plants***. That is a piece of sage advice I always give my landscape customers. If you can't afford any other landscaping this year, at least get your trees. Trees will literally double in value every year whether they are in your yard, or being shifted up to a larger pot size in my nursery. A $200 tree should increase to a $400 size next season. However, in most cases a foundation shrub that costs $20 this year will be worth about $20 next year, and the next.

On the southern and western exposures, it may be wise to plant some trees that will be large enough to produce shade. Once you live through our summers, you will appreciate the cooling effect of trees, and the concomitant reduction of air conditioning costs. On north or east facings, I like to consider trees that are more ornamental in look and stature. If you already have existing trees, give thought to removing those that block the view of the front entrance. Again, your landscaping should remain outside of the visualized funnel. Don't be overly concerned that some choices of trees will drop their leaves in the fall (deciduous trees). They produce shade when it is important, and allow solar energy to warm your house when it's cold.

Trees are vital to the planet, and vital as "bones" of your landscape. If you are mixing in some tropical plants, use landscape palms in place of some of your trees. Remember though, evergreen trees such as magnolias, live oaks and hollies fit in with more tropical foliage and give your yard more of a Gulf Coast ambiance.

Choose the corner plantings and bare wall focals next. These plants will also serve as "bones" for your landscape, and will lend your bedded areas the structure they need. You will want evergreen shrubs for your corners. I like to plant these shrubs about 3' to 4' from the house corners. They will soften the 90° angle of the corner. They also act as a "wing wall", actually making the home appear larger. And finally, the well placed evergreen corner plantings helps screen the sides of your house from the street. The sides of your home will be the least visited, the least viewed, and therefore should get the last and least landscape investment.

Corner and wall plantings should not be allowed to exceed a height of 2/3 of the eave height, so if your eave height is 9', then 6' is the height you want that shrub to attain and the height with which you want too keep it pruned. Plants growing up and enveloping the eaves of a house look overgrown and unkempt.

Repeat the use of your chosen plants throughout the yard to create symmetry and continuity in your landscape. For example, if you use a corner planting on one end of your home, try and repeat it on the other end. If you use dwarf yaupon by the front of the house, also use some by the mailbox. Repeating varieties of plants in different beds ties the landscape together. This rule applies to the front yard, or back yard, or side yard separately. Of course, you can change up plant choices completely when you move to the back yard from the front.

Blank walls and vacant spaces between windows beg for the tall accents, but many times the parameters needed may be too narrow for a wide choice of plants. Consider a trellis or an obelisk in such a circumstance. Plant a flowering vine on it, and it can become your favorite focal. Don't forget to keep it pruned to form.

Picking shrubs and color for your beds can be daunting because of the hundreds and even thousands of choices to make. The best way to choose is to narrow the field, and with a few rules you can narrow it rapidly.

A larger home with excellent curb appeal. Note especially the curving bed lines, the tall accents and the simplicity of the planting. There are no more than 8 species in the front yard.

Know the facing of your house so that you can pick sun and shade lovers appropriately. One of the biggest mistakes "do it yourselfers" make is to go into a home improvement store and start buying plants without any knowledge of the plants needs or growth habits.

The shrubs near your house should be slow growing and easy to maintain. Prime examples to avoid would be red top photinia, eleagnus, or leyland cypress. Each will fit for a few months, but even in the second growing season they can not be maintained to scale.

Your shrub choices should be primarily evergreen and dependable. It is easy to understand that if you choose a propensity of deciduous shrubs, beds will look stark and bare in the winter. You also want to take care putting in too many half-hardy tropical plants. The house may look great in summer, but if we have a hard freeze you will have to completely redo your frozen beds in the spring.

Contrast the shapes, structure, texture and color of the plants as you are choosing them. Plants that are of different species but close in terms of look should not go into the same bed. From a distance, plants that are too similar look like unhealthy specimens of the same plant.

Do not overplant your beds, i.e., not too many plants, and not too close together. I personally like to be able to appreciate each plant individually. The mulch between the plants makes them stand out in the same way you mat a picture within a picture frame.

Refrain from using too many varieties. This is especially difficult for people that love plants. They want at least one of everything. Their beds can become a hodge-podge with too many kinds of plants. Simplify and bring order to the chaos! I generally don't like to use any more than 6 to 10 species across any view of the home.

Groups of 3 and 5 plants are appealing aesthetically. I'm not sure why, but I know it's true. For whatever reason, other groupings look incomplete. Also, be careful when choosing pairs of matching plants. Plants can, and will, grow at slightly different rates, and in a pairing this difference shows up like a sore thumb.

Older homes are especially prone to having shrubs near the house that are overgrown. To prevent this, ***know to what size your plants can be pruned and maintained to that size over time.***

When deciding whether to remove plants in any older landscape consider if the plant adds to the look. ***If an existing plant <u>does not add</u> to the landscape, <u>it detracts</u>.***

Curving bedlines, focals, and contracting shapes and textures enhance this small 900 sq ft front yard.

Whatever you plant in front of windows must be kept below the window sills. Windows hidden behind hedges are not attractive.

Landscape mat, or "weed mat", should be avoided under most circumstances. Even the best mats cause the roots of shrubs to grow just under the surface, and weeds can still grow on top of the mat. The only places I advise using mat are in full sun xeroscapes where minimal plants are used, and rock mulches become the focus. I also don't like to use plastic, metal or concrete borders because they rarely look anything but artificial.

It is easy to see why this does not work. This line of ligustrums is covering the bottom of the windows. They really can't be maintained any lower. Pull them out and start over!

I do advise homeowners to ***use natural mulches***. Be sure to put them in at the right depth; about 2 inches for wood mulches, pulled away from the crown of each plant. Pine needles should go down at a depth of about 8", but over the course of several weeks it will settle into a mat of 2 inches. These mulches are beneficial to the health of your plants, and will <u>help</u> to control weeds. However, you must ***routinely weed your beds***. In 2 weeks any new bed will have 5 to 10 weeds appear. Their seeds are being dropped by birds, or are blown in the wind. If you pull those first 5 or 10 weeds, it will keep them from reseeding and turning into 30 or 40. If <u>every</u> week you will weed your beds of those few volunteers, you should not have a problem. Otherwise you will lose the battle and the war.

Having a recap of these rules, or principles, may be useful to those of you that respond better to lists than to narrative and explanations. I know I do!

- A landscape design is largely subjective.
- Design with resale in mind.
- Make bed lines curve.
- Make your beds generous and in scale with the house and lot.
- Avoid mowing difficulties with your bed lines.
- Keep your bed at least 4' wide by your house.
- You generally shouldn't plant any closer than 2' from the foundation.
- Have a focal point near the front entrance.
- Your front entrance should remain the focus.
- Do not block the front entrance with landscaping.

- Pick the trees before you choose the other plants.
- Choose the corner plantings and bare wall focals next.
- Corner and wall plantings should not be allowed to exceed a height of 2/3 of the eave height.
- Repeat the use of your chosen plants throughout the yard.
- Know the facing of your house so that you can pick sun and shade lovers appropriately.
- The shrubs near your house should be slow growing and easy to maintain.
- Your shrub choices should be primarily evergreen and dependable.
- Contrast the shapes, structure, texture and color of the plants.
- Do not over plant your beds.
- Refrain from using too many varieties.
- Groups of 3 and 5 plants are appealing aesthetically.
- Know what size your plants can be pruned and maintained over time.
- If an existing plant does not add to the landscape, it detracts.
- Whatever you plant in front of windows must be kept below the window sills.
- Landscape mat should be avoided, under most circumstances.
- Use natural mulches.
- Routinely weed your beds.

Given the chance, don't miss the opportunity to curve your drive. This drive curves gracefully and contrasts well with the St. Augustine lawn. The picture is one of a home on the Gulf Coast of Alabama.

To plan to landscape your front yard, it may be helpful to use a four step process beginning with the site plan of your home including the street, mailbox, driveway and walk, placement of front door, windows, etc.
1. In step one you will locate TREES. They are the bones of your landscape which dictate the structure, shade and views into your yard.
2. The BED LINES are the next decisions to be made. What is going to be the size and scope of your landscape? It should appear generous, but not out of scale with the home or neighborhood. All of your shrubs and color, and perhaps even some trees will go into bedded areas.
3. The FOCALS are smaller bones of your landscape. They may be small trees or palms, or large shrubs which interrupt blank walls, soften corners or draw attention to certain points.
4. The SHRUBS and FLOWERS are the last part of the planting to consider. They are filler to complete the picture that you want your home and personality to project.
What follows is a graphic representation of this four step process.

1. Trees
2. Bed lines
3. Focals
4. Shrubs and flowers

Below is a legend for the trees and shrubs used in this landscape, followed by a rationale for their use.

Live Oak - chosen to envelop this home in evergreen shade over time, as well as help to screen the eastern end of the home from traffic and street noise.

"Natchez" Crape Myrtle - will lend its white flowers in the summer, and its crimson bark in fall and winter.

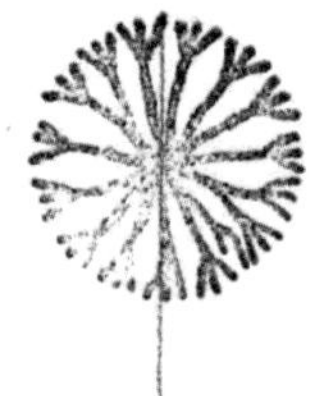

Japanese Maple - an inspiring, deciduous tree that will maintain its small stature. I chose a green leaf variety enclosed by the walk and a red leaf variety to show off behind and under the green Live Oaks.

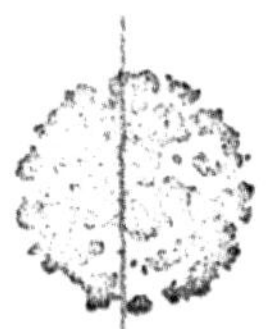

“Little Gem” Magnolia - Two are placed to the west of the drive. Their smaller structure will not outsize the 12’ strip of property in which they are planted, and who can resist Magnolia flowers up to six months per year from this evergreen variety?

Sago Palm - a focal designed to draw the eye to the front door. This can be used in traditional landscapes as well as tropical.

Japanese Yew - an evergreen focal that I like to keep pruned as 6’ columns. There are four in this landscape. Two are used to soften and fill inside corners, and the outer two are used to soften outside corners as well as act as “wing walls” to reduce the need to landscape the sides of the home.

Camellia Japonica - these two evergreen plants between the three live oaks will provide large colorful blooms during the winter months.

Holly Fern - repeated under each of the three windows, these shade lovers offer great contrast with the other broad-leafed shrubs that are used.

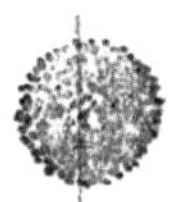

Japanese Boxwood - a light green plant that can be kept to 2’ to 2-1/2’ and can easily be uniformly maintained. They serve as a terrific foundation plant carried across the face of the home.

Southern Indica Azaleas - large growing azaleas to give spring color under the live oaks. The owners should maintain these azaleas in this situation to about 4’ x 4’.

“Knock Out” Roses - used in 2 places, at the junction of the drive and walk, and at the mailbox. The single “Knockout” rose just to the left of the garage is a patio form with a 3’ standard, topped with red blooms which will persist up to 9 months of the year.

Satsuki Gumpo Azaleas - the smallest of azalea varieties, available in white or pink. These late spring blooming 12” to 14” plants are used around the Japanese maples, as well as along the narrow bed beside the walk.

Agapanthus - used to sharply contrast with the gumpo azaleas, this variety of Agapanthus will spike a panicle of blue flowers that will reach 2-1/2’ in spring.

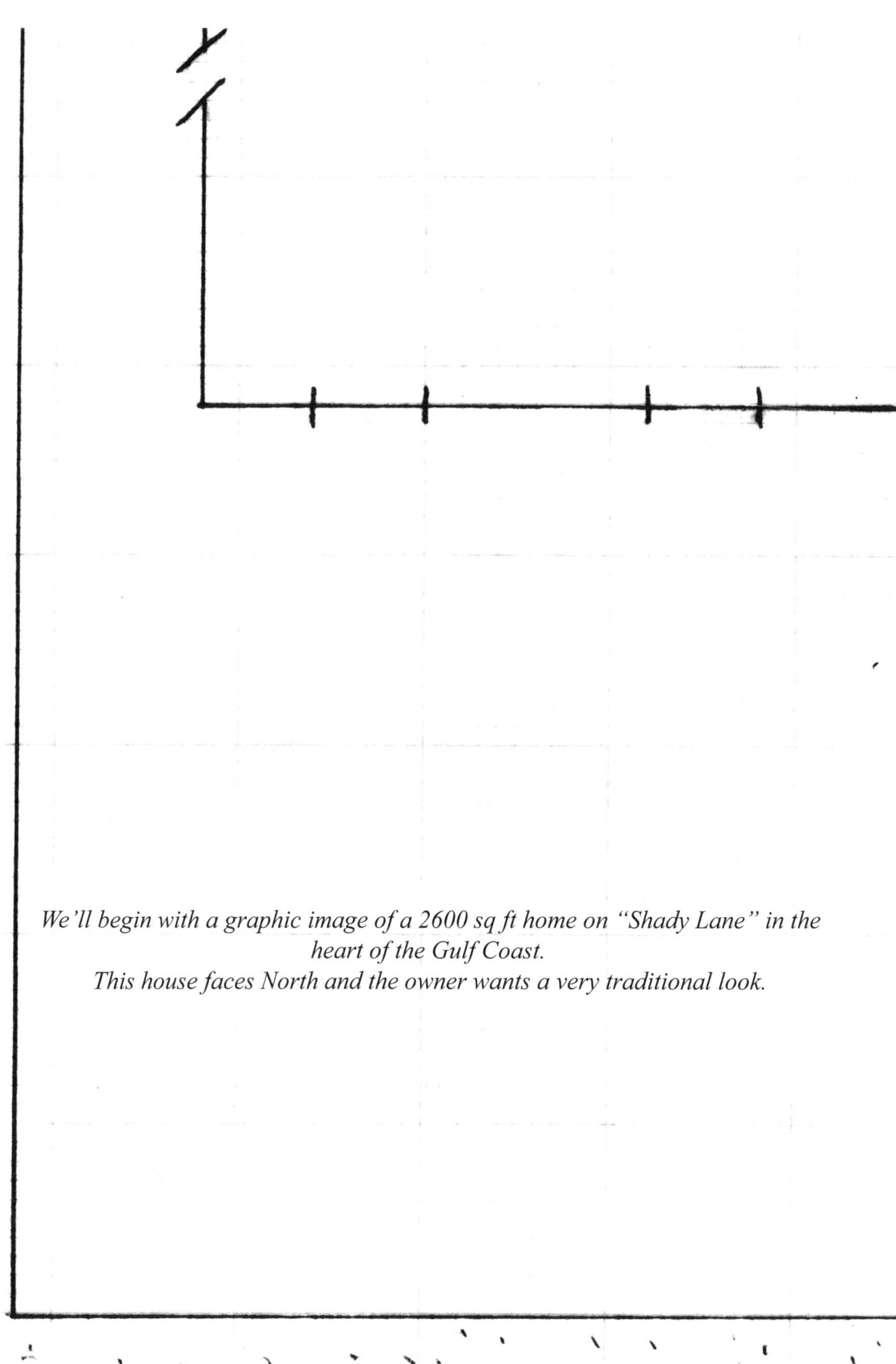

We'll begin with a graphic image of a 2600 sq ft home on "Shady Lane" in the heart of the Gulf Coast.
This house faces North and the owner wants a very traditional look.

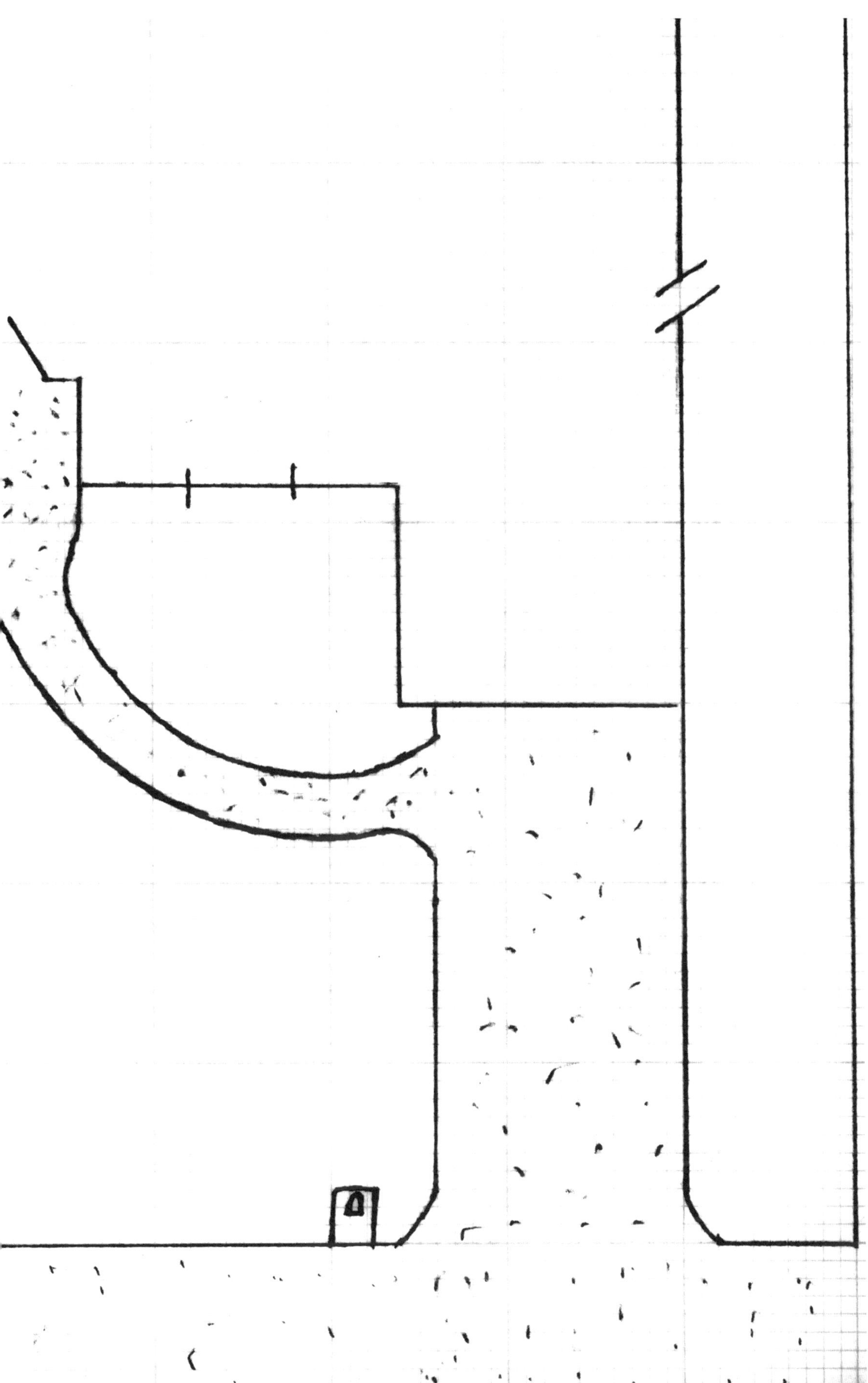

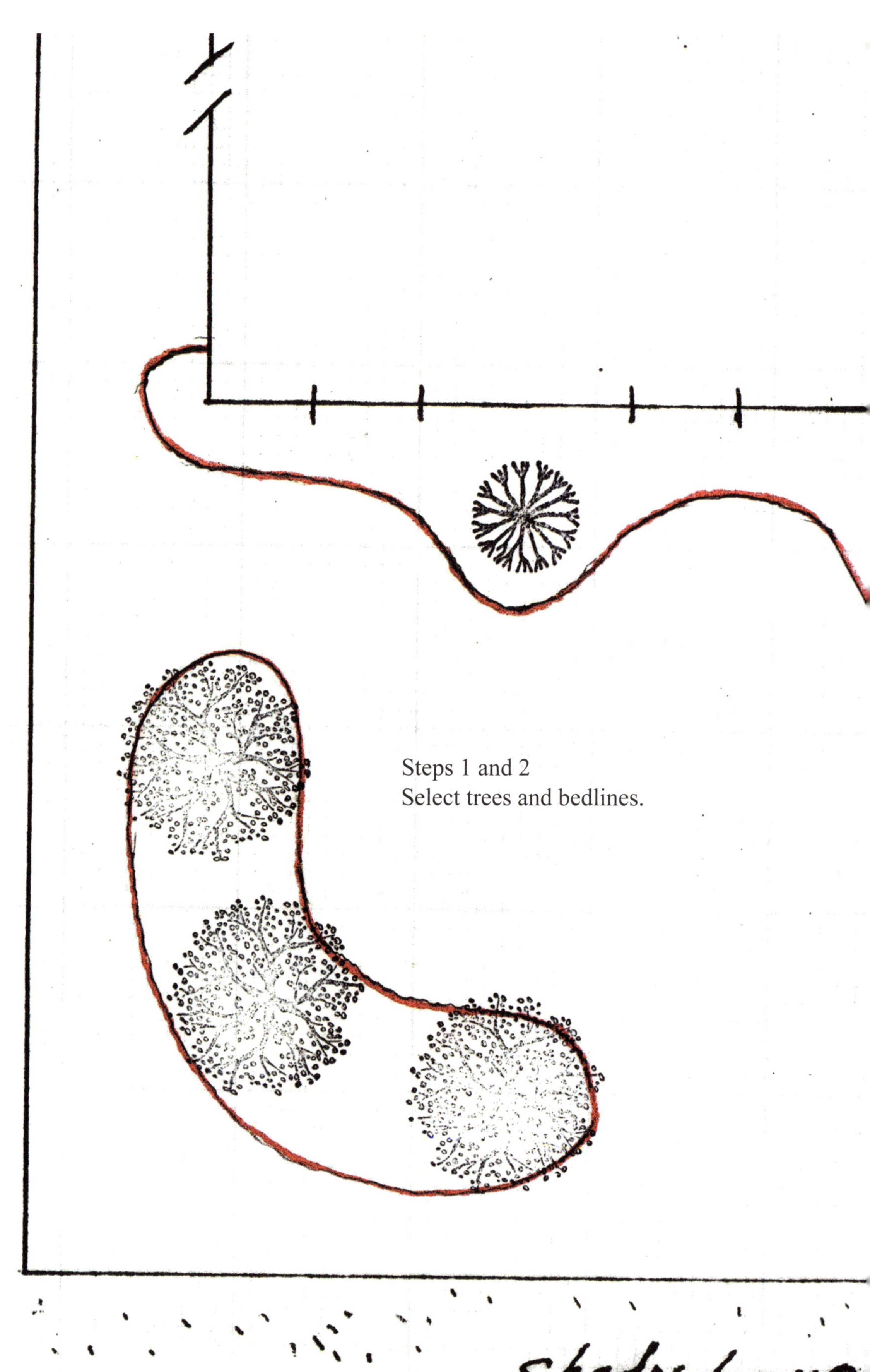

Steps 1 and 2
Select trees and bedlines.

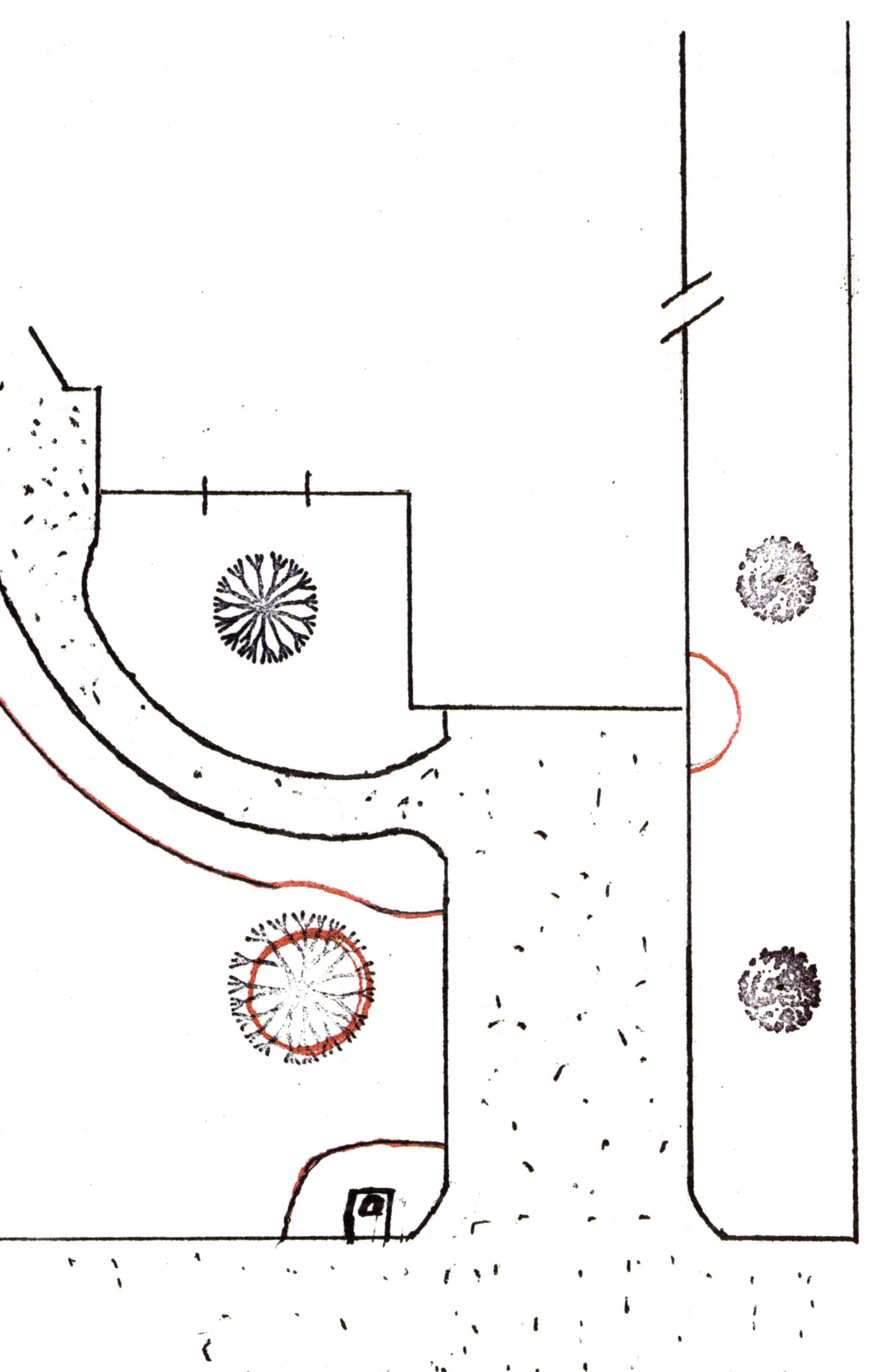

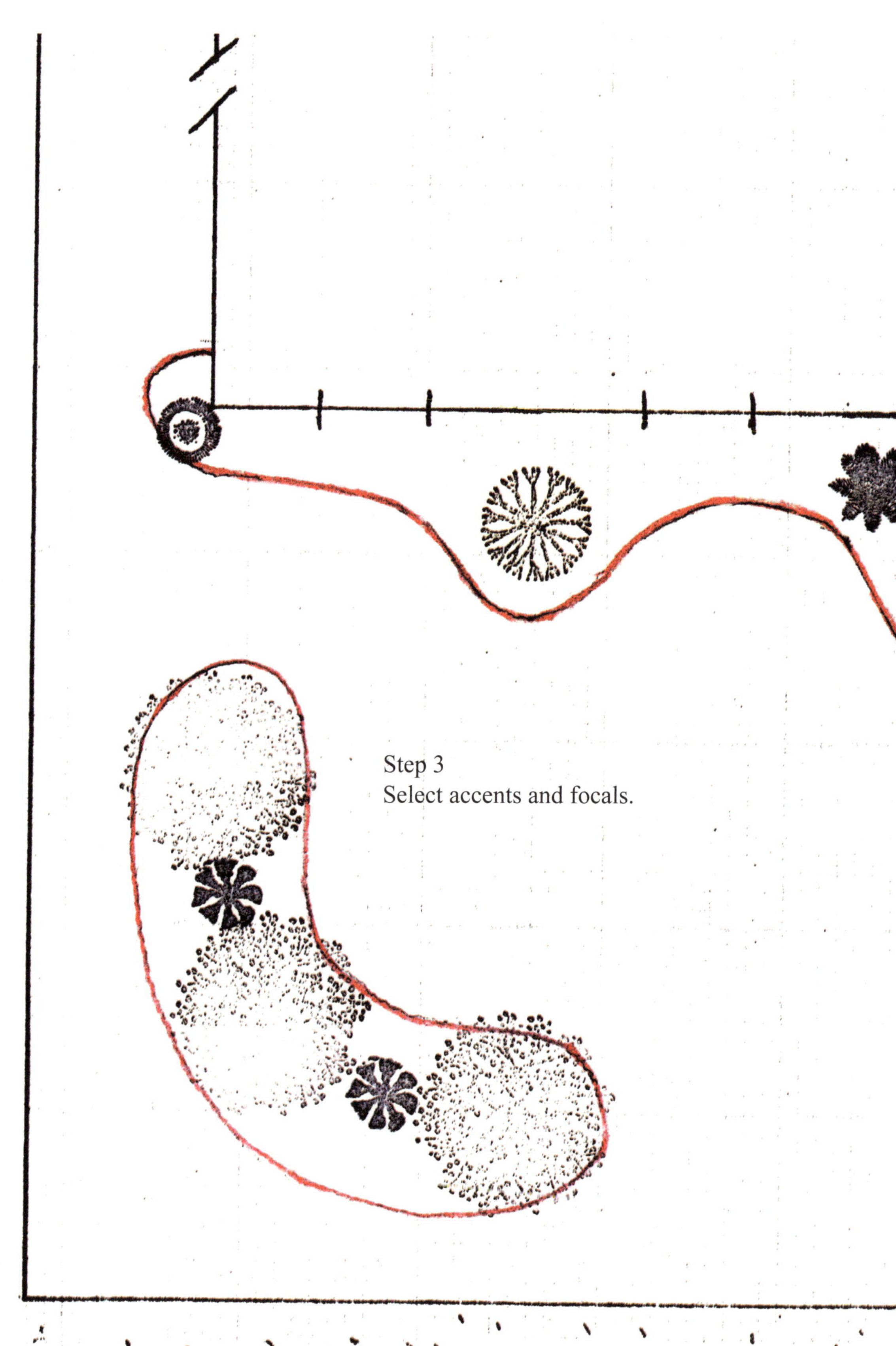

Step 3
Select accents and focals.

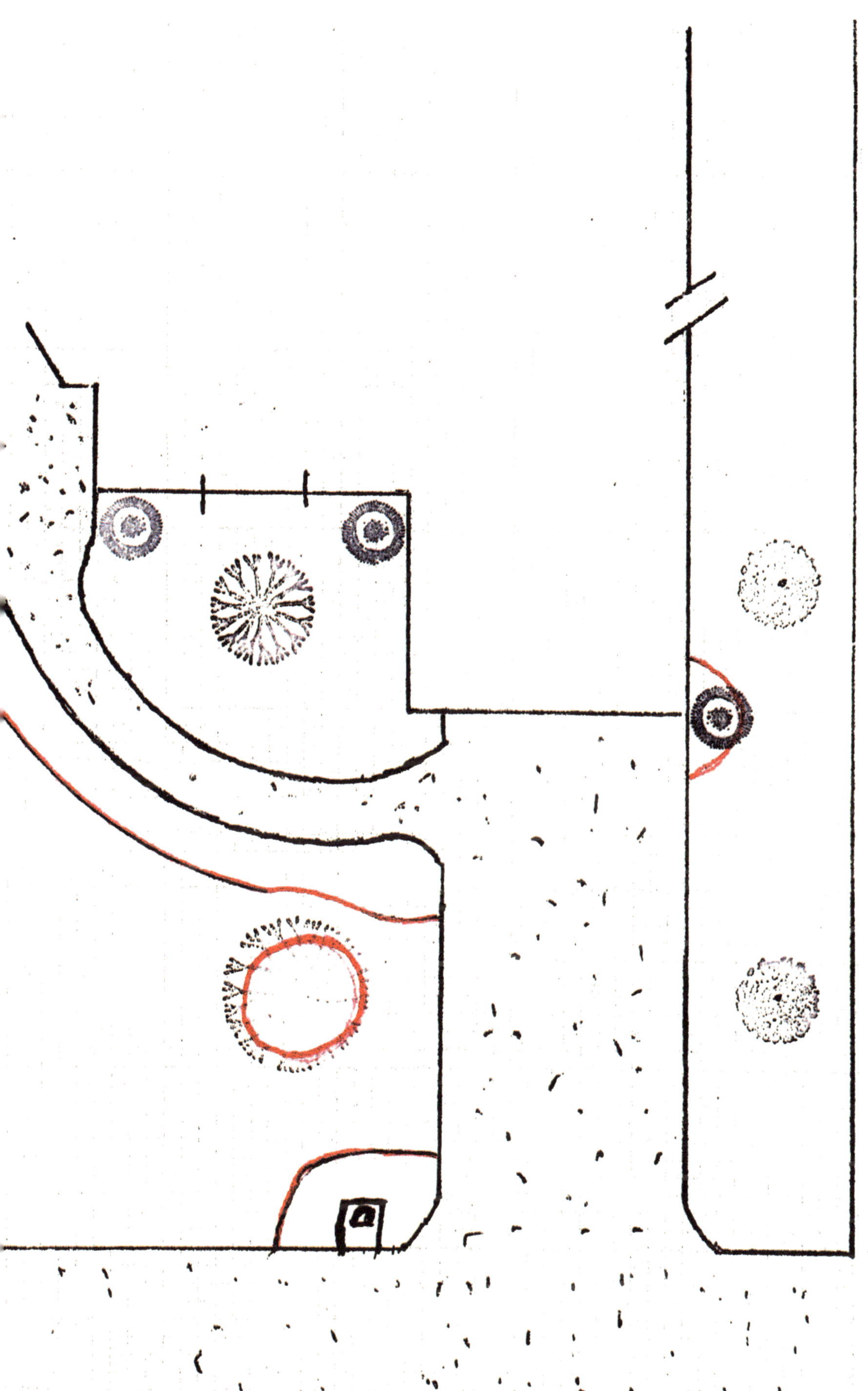

Step 4
Select shrubs and color.
Shady Lane

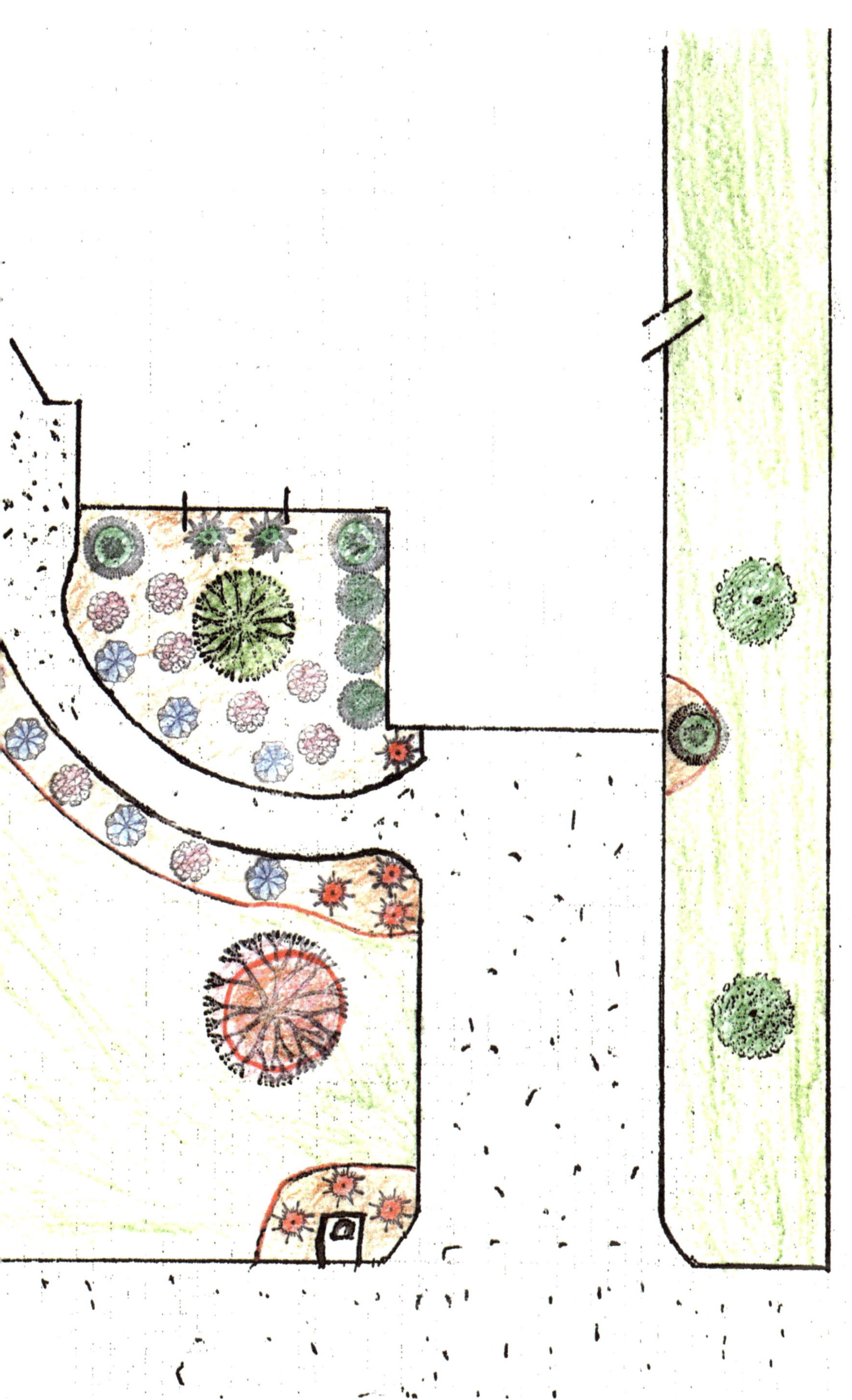

SHADE vs. SUN ENVIRONMENTS

Plants have developed certain niches over the millennia. We are aware of certain climate and weather related niches. But once those corners of the environment were filled with opportunistic plants, other species began to fill in the less desirable shaded areas. Thus the understory of ancient forests became the ancestors of our shade loving modern day plants. You have noticed that many plants that are described as sun loving in northern climates need protection from our intense summers. For example, Hostas may be used in sunny areas in New England, but are sure to fry in the sun on our Gulf Coast. That's what usually happens to shade lovers planted in too much sun. You may see the more exposed leaves lose their dark green color and become yellowish, brownish or burned looking. You may have success keeping marginal plants alive during spring, fall and winter, but summer will bring disappointment. For those plants, you need to relocate them to a shadier spot if you have a shadier spot that needs the plant. If you don't have a vacancy in the shaded parts of your yard, discard the plant. Keep your plants in perspective; they are not puppies. It is okay to toss them. Otherwise they can create a wart on the nose of your yard!

Sun lovers can be placed in too much shade. The first defensive mechanism of a shade incarcerated sun lover is literally to reach for the sun. When your normally straight plants are leaning out at a 45° angles to get to the sun, you should get the hint and move them. Plants that can take either sun or shade locations will respond accordingly. Those grown in sunny spots may have leaves that are actually smaller. The growth on branches will be shorter between points, or nodes, where new branching begins. That plant is getting plenty of sun and it results in a plant that is more compact in growth habit. That same plant grown in a more shaded situation may conversely develop larger leaves. The internodal growth (or branch growth between the leaves) is longer, resulting in a plant that is less dense and perhaps has a layered look to its foliage.

Seasons of sun and shade also matter. From Orlando, Florida and south, Impatiens are frequently planted in full sun, but only as a winter annual. Impatiens grown on the Gulf Coast must only be grown in the summer, and only in shade. Plant labels in big box stores or national gardening catalogs may not be taken for granted with respect to our Gulf Coast environment. Local gardeners, local nurseries, your local County Extension Service, and your direct observation will be a much better guide to questions of shade vs. sun. Know the microclimate of your home, and know the plant before incorporating it into your landscape. You will want your plants to thrive, not just survive.

Oleander is one of those plants that must have full sun and will take salt spray. This particular variety called "Petite Pink," grows to about 4'- 5'. It's one of my favorites.

SALT, WIND AND SAND ENVIRONMENTS

Nothing is as perplexing as choosing landscape plants for the barrier islands along our coasts. These environments also sometimes extend to peninsulas and even the mainland. But many times not! It has a great deal to do with the microclimate surrounding the home.

Salt is toxic to most plants, but weirdly beneficial to a few. Consistent wind creates a difficult environment for most plants in that it desiccates the tissues. A pure sand soil is not a desirable planting mix for most plants. Properties very near the Gulf of Mexico are therefore quite restricted in terms of plants that will thrive. Questions that I ask my barrier island customers when they are shopping for plants include, asking for their address. If I am familiar with the street, I have a better idea of proximity to the Gulf. If they are close to the Gulf, I ask if they get a film of salt spray on their windows, each or every few days. You won't see this spray, but you see the accumulation in the matter of hours or days in beach environments. That salt spray falls on foliage as well as windows.

In close proximity, up to several blocks from the coast, it is important to know if the plants are going on the windward or leeward sides of the house. Windward is toward the Gulf, and usually south. The leeward side of the home offers a good deal of protection from wind and subsequent salt spray. The size of the house is important. A large, 3 story house will block a lot more wind and salt spray than a small cottage. If a question as to suitability of the plant lingers, I will ask if their nearby neighbors have had year round success with this plant variety in this location. I have dissuaded many of my customers from experimenting with plants in these questionable circumstances. There are tried and true plants that will work even in front line salt spray situations. In the last chapter is a list of plants that we routinely plant on our local barrier island. But again, the reference to a plant being salt tolerant does not mean it will survive in front line situations. This book is not meant to be an exhaustive reference for coastal plantings. However, there are sites on the internet and in-depth publications on the subject. There are dozens of natives to our barrier islands which are available to be ordered, but most are not routinely stocked in nurseries.

Our Gulf Coast barrier islands are a national treasure. The sea oats in the foreground add splendor to our beaches and help to hold the sand in place during wind events. Sea oats not only tolerate the salt and wind, the plant must have a regular misting of salt spray to survive. Away from the coast, they will quickly succumb to fungal disease normally suppressed by salt spray, a natural fungicide.

MYTHS

For years I have heard the same myths repeated by different customers year after year. They heard what they think is gospel from their neighbor, and so the myth is spread from neighbor to neighbor. Perhaps a partial listing of common misconceptions will help.

Spring is the time to plant. Spring is a good time to plant on the Gulf Coast, but so is summer, fall and winter. Whatever is a good time for you is appreciated by any plant that lives here year round. By planting, you are removing the restriction of its roots by taking the plant out of the plastic bucket and putting it in the ground. Further north, winter is avoided because the frozen ground is too difficult to deal with. Not so, on the Gulf Coast. About 1' down the soil remains at about 60 degrees here, even on the coldest nights. If I were to have to pick a best season to install trees and shrubs it would be the fall. As temperatures drop, most plants will slow their "botanical metabolism" needing less water and nutrients. Yet their roots will continue to grow in our warm earth so that they are better prepared in spring for a new flush of foliage.

Always amend the soil when planting. We covered this misconception earlier, but to refresh your memory, don't add compost or peat to the soil when you are planting a tree or other isolated plant. It may not help, and it may be a waste of time and money. Only when an area is being bedded for installation of a variety of landscape plants and flowers is mixing in soil amendments recommended.

When you transplant a tree or shrub; prune it heavily to make up for the root loss. Not so fast! Chemicals in the ends of branches signal the plant to grow more roots. Cut the signal, and you may stifle root regeneration. Occasionally you may need to prune a transplant, but if you can avoid it, do so.

Always use a sealer on bark wounds or exposed large pruning cuts. It really does no good. Spray it only if you think it makes the plant look better.

When you prune a tree, leave a short length of limb attached to the trunk. Supposedly this myth is perpetuated by those that think that otherwise the tree may "bleed" to death. There is a proper place to trim, or prune, limbs from trees. It is just in front of the collar, or swelling, where the branch connects to the trunk of the tree. The pruning cut made in the correct place will actually seal over time. But the cut has to be made correctly. Too far out and the specialized tissue can not reach the wound. Too close in and you are removing the tissue that is capable of sealing the cut.

Construction is safe for a tree as long as the area under the drip line is not disturbed. Construction anywhere within about twice the drip line of a tree can be detrimental and even fatal to a tree, and the damage or death may not occur until up to seven years later. Many times roots extend far beyond the drip line. If the area over the roots is scraped, or soil is added to it, the tree is adversely affected.

Add soil to the top of the root ball of a new planting to be sure the roots are well covered. On the contrary, roots that are established have an air exchange as well as a water exchange. Burying roots too deep can cause the plant great stress as it tries to reestablish the correct level of its roots. Another problem attributed to planting too deeply is a rot that can develop in the bark that is now submerged in soil. More trees and shrubs are probably lost to this mistake by homeowners than any other. Always plant so that the top of the root ball is level with the surrounding grade.

Water your grass once per day about 15 minutes. No! No! No! Water deeply, but infrequently. That means ¾" to 1" every time you water, but only when the grass needs it. See a previous chapter for specifics. Frequent, light waterings will result in a weed infested, bug damaged and diseased lawn. I promise you.

Cut your grass short to choke out weeds. Grasses need to be maintained at a specific height for the grass blades to produce enough food for the plant, (at least 3" for St. Augustine, and at least 2" for centipede). Our new grasses compete very effectively with weeds if the grasses are given a chance.

The right grass will grow in heavy shade. There is not a lawn grass that will thrive in heavy shade. Bed those areas in heavy shade and plant them with shade lovers.

There are new miracle grasses, like Zoyzia, that need less maintenance. Wrong! St. Augustine cultivars and centipede are the best grasses for the Gulf Coast. I truly think that the best lawns are a mixture of St. Augustine cultivars and centipede. May the fittest survive! In patches that become sparse, plug in a different cultivar.

Add lime once per year. Lime raises the pH of your soil. Depending on the existing pH of your soil and the particular plant or lawn grass you want to grow, you may be doing more harm than good. Our Gulf Coast soils are generally in the acidic range, and most of the plants and grasses we strive to grow here prefer it that way. Only if you have had problem areas that won't grow what you want to grow should you suspect a pH problem, and only then should you need to have your soil tested. And only with a recommendation should you attempt to raise or lower your soil's pH.

All fertilizers are the same. Buy the cheapest. It never ceases to amaze me how many people will try and save money by buying the wrong, but cheap fertilizer for their lawn that costs thousands of dollars to install. Good fertilizers today are formulated for specific plants. They have slow release formulations and the right amount of N.P.K., plus numerous micronutrients. There is not one fertilizer that is good for all of your plants any more than there is one pet food that will sustain all of your pets. If you feed your cat a steady diet of hamster food, it will develop nutritional deficiencies. So will your plants.

A little fertilizer is good, but more is better. Read the labels on the package. Too much fertilizer can defoliate your plant, streak your lawn, or kill either. At the least, new overly succulent foliage is more susceptible to insect damage.

With the right chemicals you can have a weed free lawn. Chemicals may help you with as much as 10% of your lawn problems, but correct cultural practices (watering, mowing and fertilizing) will help you with the other 90%.

If you need to kill bugs, get the strongest thing available. 98% of the insects that you see are either neutral or even beneficial to your plants, *think honey bees and ladybugs*. Insecticides should be selected only to control the damaging insects that you have first identified in your plants. Insects, like all other groups of animals, have an important place in our environment. Be ever so cautious when using insecticides. First try controlling infestations by other means such as trying to improve air circulation around the plant, or removing infested portions. Next try natural means such as predator insects, (think praying mantis or ladybugs), or biologicals such as B.t. or *Bacillus thuringiensis*. Be kind to our planet. The others we know of don't seem nearly as hospitable.

WIND EVENTS

Visitors to the Gulf Coast may take notice of our trees being shorter than trees of the same species further inland. Until 1995 I would always explain away our lack of very tall trees based on the very sandy soil composition, and perhaps the rapid leaching of nutrients from the soil. In 1995 my part of the Gulf Coast suffered a direct hit by two hurricanes, Erin (category 1) and Opal (Category 3). This was my first hurricane experience, and during the first one I had a horticultural and physics epiphany. The taller a tree, the more leverage the wind has to blow it over! If you are a tree that stands taller than your neighbor you are subject to the destructive forces of probably the Gulf Coast's worst characteristic, periodic hurricanes! Hurricane Camille struck the Mississippi in 1969 with sustained winds of 190 m.p.h., making it a very strong category 5. Since then our Gulf Coast has endured eight other major (category 3 and above) hurricanes, including Katrina (category 3) that devastated New Orleans and the Mississippi and Alabama Gulf Coast in 2005.

Saffir Simpson Hurricane Scale

Cat 1	Winds 74 - 95	Surge 4 - 5 feet
Cat 2	Winds 96 – 110	Surge 6 – 8 feet
Cat 3	Winds 111 – 130	Surge 9 – 12 feet
Cat 4	Winds 131 – 155	Surge 13 – 19 feet
Cat 5	Winds above 155	Surge greater than 18 feet

Left: The sign and reader board at my nursery one day before Hurricane Ivan struck in 2004.
Right: The sign the day after.

Hurricanes are not the only threat. We have tropical storms and some strong, straight line winds in usual non-tropical thunderstorms. Virtually every year I have lived here, our trees are threatened by winds of 30 to 40 m.p.h.. So your tree's wind tolerance should become a factor when planning your landscape.

Here are some useful tips when planning your landscape for high wind tolerance. Keep in mind, however, that storms may not recognize your best efforts, and you can only hope to minimize inevitable damage in a major hurricane.

Trees that grew in a forest environment and have had their neighbors removed in construction efforts are quite vulnerable. Several factors are important here. Forests of trees protect each other by breaking and slowing the wind on each individual. Now that one or only several trees remain in your yard makes them less wind tolerant. Another factor in this scenario is that construction of your house damages the root system of existing trees that may be within a distance of 50 feet of the construction. The roots, of course, support the trees during wind events. Conversely, trees grown in an unaltered environment after the house was built will fare better in storms.

I personally believe it is impossible to give a wind tolerance grade to every tree, but there are some that are weaker than others. For example, you may want to avoid numbers of:

- Ornamental Pears ("Bradford" or "Capitol Select") - Their branch structure is pretty but breaks easily.
- Indian Hawthorn trees ("Majestic Beauty" or "Rosalinda") - Those pruned into 8' to 10' tree form
- Wax Myrtle – A native that easily breaks but seems to regenerate itself sometimes from the ground after the storm
- Fast growing, deciduous shade trees, especially tall ones with extensive foliage forming a large wind resistant canopy
- Short needle Pines – May stay up during strong winds, but may die shortly after because the interior wood has been damaged
- Leyland Cypress – A man made cross that has very dense foliage supported by what may become an insufficient root structure
- Sweet Bay Magnolia – Another native tree that will break or become easily uprooted. Since their habitat is usually wet, they will re-root if necessary and generate a generous amount of new foliage after the storm.

Make no mistake though, trees in the correct place and of the right species can protect your home. At the top of that list is the State Tree of Florida:

- Sabal Palm – Anchored by a great cluster of very strong individual roots that may grow to 20' in length. The fronds of the Sabal are designed to turn with the wind and spill it quickly. The trunks are quite strong, and once established can protect buildings from wind blown debris, other falling trees, and even flotsam in storm surges.
- Other palms – Most all other palms suffer storms particularly well, perhaps because they are much older on the evolutionary scale than many other plants. They lived through stormier times in past ages, and have evolved a tolerance for wind events.
- Southern Magnolias – Native to the entire Gulf Coast, its very substantial root systems can support a large, strong canopy.
- Live Oak – What would the Gulf Coast be without live oaks and magnolias? Older live oaks many times develop low limbs that reach the ground and help to buttress the tree from the effects of wind. Old live oaks are not known for great height, but are renowned for great girth and branch spread low to the ground.
- Holly trees – such as Savannah, East Palatka, Nellie R. Stevens, Mary Nell and East Bay Hollies are all slow to moderate growers that develop strong wood and strong roots. They are rarely so large that they will threaten a structure, but can protect it in a storm.
- Crape Myrtles – These trees stand up amazingly well to storms. They are never too large to threaten a structure, but can protect it in a storm.

I have 7 crape myrtles in my yard, and 12 Sabal palms around my home.

What can you do for your particular landscape to minimize damage? In the Spring before the start of hurricane season on June 1, have your large trees pruned and shaped by an arborist. You can remove up to 1/3 of the canopy of a tree without harming it. That reduction will make a huge difference in the survivability of the tree in a strong wind event. It is always better to surgically remove limbs than to have them break during a storm.

I'm a strong believer in leaving trees that have withstood hurricanes over the years. If they have been tested in storms of category 1 – 3, why take them down? Doing so will only make remaining trees more vulnerable.

Staking small patio trees such as a rose tree, etc., is useful prior to a storm. Staking a newly planted tree prior to a hurricane is not a good idea. It is better for the newly planted tree to lean in the storm and spill the wind. Good staking can result in the trunk breaking. You can always straighten a leaning tree.

After the storm, do straighten your trees quickly if possible. They will be re-growing new roots within 6 weeks. If an older, larger tree is leaning severely you should probably remove it and start over with another. Badly broken and damaged trees should be removed. It can take them years to recover and they may never be an asset to your landscape again.

Wait for several weeks after the storm to have badly damaged trees removed if they are not a threat to people or property. Over time the prices drop dramatically for tree removal following a storm, plus after a period of time you should be able to find a competent local arborist to do the work.

Trees came down into the nursery stock, the shade house was destroyed, the tool shed was destroyed and a tractor trailer of pine straw tipped over. What a mess!

Residential streets that had been flooded in the storm surge of Ivan the week after the storm lined with drywall, furniture, mattresses, appliances and other debris.

These two pictures were taken along Mississippi's Gulf Coast. Hurricane Katrina in 2005 flooded large parts of New Orleans that were actually below sea level. That got most of the national press but Coastal Mississippi really bore the brunt of the storm. Winds are always stronger to the east of the storm's eye when they strike the Gulf Coast. The eye of Katrina went ashore just east of New Orleans putting the majority of the storm's physical wrath directly on the three coastal counties of Mississippi. The top picture is of a live oak that valiantly survived huge winds and a huge storm surge. The bottom picture is also of a live oak. It also made it through the storm with the help of an artist. All along the median of US Route 90, oaks that were too battered were left rooted and carved into dolphins and other wild residents.

These two pictures were taken along the Gulf Coast in Pass Christian, Mississippi. The top photo is of an oak tree that is several hundred years old. It stood in the front yard of a home entirely removed from its foundation by Katrina. The tree, even though hollowed by age and disease, even though battered by historic storms, still shows its life in its one remaining branch. If this old man could talk, the stories he could tell.

The bottom photo is representative of the strong will of the homeowners of Mississippi's Gulf Coast. This rebuilt home exudes the grace and hospitality of the coastal south. The only pre-Katrina landscape that remained are the two Canary Island Date Palms. Note the 15° lean, a reminder of the past and the promise of the future.

PALMS AND CYCADS

The limiting factor for the vast majority of the world's palms grown on the Gulf Coast is cold. That factor alone limits hardiness zone 9 to perhaps 20 species and zones 8b and 8a even further to perhaps 12 to 15. Cycads evolved on a more tropical earth perhaps 280 million years ago, followed closely by palms. Both groups are monocots which include such varied plants as banana plants, grasses and lilies. In monocots the tissues are bundled. In dicots, which evolved later (think live oaks, maples, magnolias, etc.) the tissues are specialized with wood, or xylem, and bark, or phloem.

Neither palms nor cycads can be pruned to be made shorter. Palms only grow from the apical meristem, or "bud", at the top of the plant where new growth continuously emerges during warm weather. If the bud freezes or dies from some other cause, the palm stalk also dies. On clustering palms, a single trunk can die without affecting the others, however. As palms and cycads grow they should be pruned and cleaned from the bottom to remove dead or dying fronds. Cycads and clustering palms can really detract from your landscape if not cleaned at least annually. A word of caution is in order however. Many times homeowners and landscapers are a bit overzealous when pruning palms. A general rule of thumb is to only remove dead fronds and those that hang below 9 and 3 o'clock. Over pruning can harm or disfigure your palm in the long run. Some arborescent palms such as large Washington palms can be left with a natural "skirt" of dead fronds and still look good. Learn from your nurseryman how to appropriately maintain your palms and cycads in a structurally groomed manner.

Our Gulf Coast tolerant palms can be easily identified verbally by knowing the color of the fronds, the shape of the fronds, and the armaments on the petiole. The shade of green in color is probably self evident. The frond shape will be described in three different ways: 1) Pinnate, or feather-like. Remember the early writing pens were quills or feathers. 2) Palmate, shaped like the palm of our hand. 3) Costapalmate, or palmate shape in which the petiole extends into the flat leaf giving it a distinct mid-rib. Most palms have developed sharp spines, spikes or teeth along the petiole which certainly are there to dissuade animals from grazing too close to that sensitive bud or newly emerging seed heads.

Palms and cycads are either monoecious or dioecious. Plants with male and female flower parts on the same plant are monoecious, and conversely when the plant is dioecious the plants are either male or female. For the most part, this hardly matters, but for the cycad, *Cycas revoluta* or sago palm, questions always arise from owners of the older specimens. I will address that on the Sago page. Adults only please!

Palms readily show nutritional deficiencies since they continuously grow during warmer months. Fertilize with a balanced fertilizer especially formulated for palms beginning March 15 each year, with a last fertilization about September 15. People attracted to move to the Gulf Coast are usually attracted to palms. Over the years I have seen a huge increase in demand for palms, including some that are marginal in their hardiness. But with so few upsides to global warming, perhaps increasing palm culture is the way to go!

My Favorite Landscape Palms

This section is intended to be but a synopsis of palms that I use in various landscape applications. There are other palms listed in other books as suitable for the Gulf Coast. At meetings of Palm Societies, members will swoon over these lesser known species and lament that the public and nursery trade doesn't appreciate their beauty and worth. Yes, there are more species that can be planted here, but I am unsure they will ever improve landscape aesthetics to a great degree. These species also may not be widely available. If you decide to explore other varieties you might want to join a Palm Society. Many of the members are avid collectors and would love to share their horticultural experiences with you.

NEEDLE PALM

Scientific name: *Rhapidophyllum hystrix*
Hardy to: Zone 7, may be the most cold hardy palm known
Habit: Clustering
Height: to 6’ Spread: to 8’+
Color: Deep green
Leaf: Palmate, deeply divided
Petiole: Smooth, however armed at base of plant with long sharp spines that look like sewing needles
Salt tolerance: Moderate
Shade Tolerance: Full sun to shade
Origin: Native to U.S. East Coast to New Jersey, also our Gulf Coast

This native clumping palm is useful as a specimen, or when planted in large groupings for a dramatic effect. At a distance you might confuse it with saw palmetto or sabal minor, but when you get pierced by one of their spines you will know it’s a needle palm.

Needle Palm - Potted for sale at my nursery. Note the needles that emerge from the base of the trunk.

SAW PALMETTO

Scientific name: *Serenoa repens*
Hardy to: Zone 8a
Habit: Clustering
Height: to 6’+ in right conditions
Spread: unlimited as a colonizer
Color: Both a light green form and a blue green form exist
Leaf: Deeply divided palmate
Petiole: Finely toothed on edge
Salt tolerance: High – found in native state on barrier islands
Shade tolerance: Full sun to shade
Origin: Native to lower southern coastal plain of U.S.

Saw Palmetto - This green leaf variety as opposed to the silver leaf variety is an easily recognized native on the gulf coast..

This interesting native plant is easy to maintain, very tough and quite attractive in the right parts of your yard. The trunks are primarily horizontal and grow just under the ground. Too many times contractors will remove them as a nuisance in new landscapes. Replacing them is expensive, and their growth is slow. They do not transplant easily. Buy them in pots grown from seed. Bring lots of money, and lots of patience!

DWARF PALMETTO, DWARF SABAL

Scientific name: *Sabal minor*
Hardy to: Zone 7
Habit: Solitary single crown with foliage only, rarely visible trunk
Height: to 6' Spread: to 6'
Color: non-distinguishing green
Leaf: New leaves arrive palmate, but older ones develop shortly costapalmate structure
Petiole: Smooth
Salt tolerance: Moderate
Shade tolerance: Shade to full sun
Origin: Southeastern U.S.

A solitary, non-arborescent palm native to the Gulf Coast that prefers an understory situation, but will take full sun. Useful as specimens in shaded areas where few other palms would grow. Not often seen in landscapes, and not often available in commercial trade.

Dwarf Palmetto - Not a very exciting palm, but it is one of our few natives. Distinguish it from Saw Palmetto by its lack of small teeth on the petiole.

EUROPEAN FAN PALM, MEDITERANEAN FAN PALM

Scientific name: *Chamaerops humilis*
Hardy to: Zone 8a
Habit: A clumping non-arborescent
Height: to 8'+
Spread: Single trunk to 5'
Color: Light green with white fuzz-like texture toward center of leaf
Leaf: Palmate, deeply divided
Petiole: Heavily armed with narrow sharp spikes
Salt tolerance: Moderate
Shade tolerance: Full sun
Origin: The Mediteranean region

European Fan Palm - These clumps of European Fan Palms, located around the statue of Andrew Jackson in Jackson Square in New Orleans, are beautifully groomed. My lovely wife is posed beside the palm to show the scale of these magnificent specimens. This author knows of no other European Fan Palms on the Gulf Coast that have reached this size.

This is an excellent cold hardy addition to a sunny Gulf Coast landscape. The form will be dictated by your skill at pruning. Normally budding new shoots at a main trunk, they can be kept beautifully structured as a multi-trunk by leaving the main trunk and 3 uniformly spaced inferior trunks pruned up to show off their form. They can also make an attractive single trunk specimen by keeping the lesser shoots pruned away at the base of the main trunk. Left alone they will revert to their natural colonizing appearance which is unkempt and difficult to regain control of due to the skin piercing armaments. Prune at least twice per year.

LADYFINGER PALM
Scientific name: *Rhapis excelsa*
Hardy to: Zone 9
Habit: Dense clustering palm
Height: to 8'   Spread: A dense colonizer
Color: Dark green in shade, lighter in sun
Leaf: Deeply divided palmate, blunted tips
Petiole: Very thin, unarmed
Salt Tolerance: Mild
Shade tolerance: Shade preferred
Origin: China

Along the Gulf Coast, this palm is usually sold and used as a very durable house plant. Trunks are quite thin, perhaps 1" – 2" in diameter and covered with brown fibrous material. Makes an interesting addition to a shady zone 9 microclimate.

Ladyfinger palm planted against the fence is protected from the north winds of winter and enjoys a shaded location.

CHINESE FAN PALM
Scientific name: *Livistonia chinensis*
Hardy to: Zone 9
Habit: Clustering foliage when young, will develop primary single trunk when older
Height: to 20'   Spread: 8' single trunk
Color: Light Kelly green
Leaf: Palmate when young, costapalmate when older
Petiole: Armed on lower half with sharp spikes
Salt tolerance: Moderate
Shade tolerance: Shade to full sun
Origin: China

A true chameleon of form. It is usually purchased as a container of foliage emerging from different places on the soil surface. Over perhaps several years the plant will remain a clump of tropical light green foliage. After a period of years though, a dominant trunk will emerge and this clump of palmate foliage will turn into an arborescent palm with costapalmate foliage. Be sure to plant where the transition can occur without causing problems. A closely related species is the Ribbon Palm, or *Livistonia dicipiens*. It is reportedly a bit more cold hardy than its *chinensis* cousin.

Chinese Fan Palm - This specimen stands in the corner of a yard in New Orleans.

PYGMY DATE PALM

Scientific Name: *Phoenix roebelenii*
Hardy to: Zone 10
Habit: Clustering
Height: to 8'
Spread: Single trunk to 5'
Color: Glossy green
Leaf: Pinnate
Petiole: Sharply armed with thin spines at base
Salt Tolerance: Low
Shade Tolerance: Full sun
Origin: Southeast Asia

Pygmy Date Palm shown silhouetted on a bare wall.

This little cousin of the larger Date Palm seduces many landscape enthusiasts along the Gulf Coast. In its grandest splendor, it is sold as a 3 trunk specimen with feathery fronds that move in the breeze and just beg to be the focus of everyone's front entrance. But buyer beware! They are largely unsuited for our regular cold snaps and will die when their temperature reaches 25 degrees or below. Only if you have a courtyard situation within a mile or so of the Gulf, or a heat trapping alcove facing south or east should you try this palm.

SAGO PALM

Scientific name: *Cycas revoluta*
Hardy to: Zone 8
Habit: Solitary if kept groomed, a chaotic colonizer otherwise
Height: to 12'+ Spread: to 9'+
Color: Dark bottle green
Leaf: Pinnate with stiff leaflets
Petiole: Short, armed with short spikes
Salt tolerance: Moderate
Shade tolerance: Shade to full sun
Origin: Asia & Africa

A Sago by the entrance serves as a warm Gulf Coast greeting.

Sagos make an excellent addition to a Gulf Coast landscape. When used as a focal near the entrance, they are reminiscent of a pineapple that is used as a welcome in the Hawaiian Islands. When used on our Gulf Coast it will bridge the tropical and traditional landscape. There are 2 mistakes novice homeowners make with their sagos, however; they plant them too close to walks, walls, drives or other plants. Be sure to allow for a 9' to 10' spread. Also, sagos have to be maintained at least annually. Pups, or new starts at the base, have to be removed and older lower foliage should be removed. Sagos reproduce in two ways. First they bud at their base, trying to colonize and spread. Secondly they reproduce by producing pollen and seed. Interestingly the sexes are separate in sagos, thus they are dioecious, where most palms are monoecious. A mature female produces a structure in its center every summer which resembles a basketball. As the structure matures in a matter of weeks it will unveil numerous red seeds about the size of pecans. The male produces an erect structure in its center, called a strobilus. The strobilus resembles, well, a male part! These reproductive structures can be removed at any time and should be removed as they mature to keep the Sago groomed.

SABAL PALM, PALMETTO PALM, CABBAGE PALM

Scientific name: *Sabal palmetto*
Hardy to: Zone 8
Habit: Solitary and arborescent
Height: to 40'+
Spread: to 10'
Color: Light to dark green
Leaf: costapalmate
Petiole: unarmed
Salt tolerance: High
Shade tolerance: Moderate shade to full sun
Origin: Native to Gulf Coast, Florida peninsula and Atlantic Coast to North Carolina.

Sabal Palm - On the shore of St. Joe Bay in Gulf County Florida, two sabals in their native environment frame the picture.

A widely planted, slow growing, highly adaptable palm. It is probably the least expensive plant per pound since it is not grown for the nursery trade, but rather harvested out of native stands and transplanted into cultured landscapes. Homeowners will find them available at nurseries both "slick" and "booted." Naturally most Sabals retain their petiole bases for many years. When these trimmed bases are left on, the palm is called booted. When the boots are absent or artificially removed, they are slick. I personally prefer the booted look, and having planted hundreds of each, my experience has shown that the booted have a higher livability rate. Interestingly, Sabal palm roots die once they are cut, unlike many other palms which regenerate roots from the cut ends. The Sabals therefore must regenerate a whole new root system once transplanted. They tend to establish poorly in wet, poorly drained soils, but will thrive in those soils if they become established. A big mistake that many homeowners make is allowing too much foliage to be pruned every year. Remove only the brown, dead foliage to keep your palm healthy. They look particularly good planted as groups of 3 or 5, and left booted blend well into a native landscape of pines and hardwoods.

QUEEN PALM, FEATHER PALM

Scientific name: *Syagrus romanzoffiana*
Hardy to: Zone 9b
Habit: Solitary, arborescent
Height: to 25'+ Spread: to 10'
Color: Dark green
Leaf: Pinnate
Petiole: unarmed
Salt Tolerance: Light
Shade tolerance: Full sun
Origin: South America

This palm looks quite like a handful of giant green peacock feathers! While suited only for the warmest wind protected microclimates of the Gulf Coast, it makes a dramatic addition to the landscape. Once established, its growth rate, potentially several feet per year, is surprising. The Queen palm is a fussy feeder and must be kept suitably fertilized to keep its color and full gossamer foliage. The trunk on a young plant resembles only tightly packed fronds, but over several years forms a hard, woody round trunk.

Queen Palm - This single specimen becomes a bisecting focal for a French Quarter Duplex.

PINDO PALM, JELLY PALM

Scientific name: *Butia capitata*
Hardy to: Zone 8
Habit: Solitary, arborescent
Height: to 15'+ Spread: to 12'
Color: Glaucous or gray green
Leaf: Pinnate
Petiole: No obvious armaments, but a sharp ragged edge to the petiole
Salt tolerance: Moderate to high
Shade Tolerance: Partial shade to full sun
Origin: South America

A widely planted palm along the Gulf Coast. Should be planted as a solitary specimen. With its long sweeping branches, the pindo's second common name is derived from the jelly that can be made from the orange ripe seed which appears in late summer. Occasionally this palm is seen as a hybrid mixing with a queen palm (*Syagrus romanzoffiana*) It is less gossamer, being upright in habit. The variability of pindos is obvious even without hybridization. Some will develop much thicker trunks, some will have longer branching, and the color is also variable among individuals.

Pindo Palm - A grouping of three Pindos. Their glaucous coloring and weeping foliage really stand out. They are perhaps better used aesthetically as single solitary specimens.

WINDMILL PALM

Scientific name: *Trachycarpus fortunei*
Hardy to: Zone 7
Habit: Solitary, arborescent
Height: to 20' Spread: 4' to 5'
Color: Dark green in ideal situations
Leaf: Palmate
Petiole: Unarmed
Salt Tolerance: Moderate
Shade tolerance: Prefers shade, will take full sun
Origin: China

Windmill Palm - This Windmill Palm located on St Charles Avenue in New Orleans offers passers-by a whimsical smile. Note the well-maintained bamboo screen behind the palm which helps create courtyard privacy for this home.

This delicate palm is easily recognizable by its slender trunk which looks like it is wrapped in brown burlap. In its native state, it is largely found in understory situations protected from harsh sun and wind. While many times listed as a palm good for salt spray environments, it is not a good barrier island selection. Not only does it not perform as well in full sun environments, its fronds are ravaged in windy environments. I personally believe that windmills prefer a clay based soil also. Numbers of specimens have been planted in Charlotte, NC. There, even in zones 7 and 8, they grow faster and healthier in the red clay of piedmont North Carolina. Visitors to Buchart Gardens in Victoria, British Columbia have long marveled at the very healthy windmills growing there. Along the Gulf Coast, choose a partially shaded, wind protected spot. Make sure the soil is well drained. Near to the house a windmill is sure to lend a delicate air of the Orient.

MEXICAN FAN PALM, WASHINGTON PALM

Scientific name: *Washingtonia robusta*
Hardy to: Zone 8b
Habit: Solitary, arborescent
Height: to 40'+ Spread: to 8'
Color: Deep green
Leaf: Palmate (with a slight fold)
Petiole: Armed with what resemble sharp curved shark's teeth

Salt tolerance: Moderate
Shade tolerance: Full sun
Origin: Mexico
Unhybridized, this widely planted palm maintains its slender trunk of 1' to 1 ½' diameter and attains impressive heights in a relatively short time. However many, if not most, *Washingtonia robusta* sold in nurseries are hybridized with its more massive cousin, *filifera*. The top leaves of this palm can be discolored or even severely scorched in our coldest winters, but in a more tropical landscape the Mexican fan palm makes a great addition. They are easy to prune until they are beyond stepladder reach. At that point, allowing them to retain the natural skirt of dead fronds is a perfectly acceptable option.

Mexican Fan Palm - "Washingtonia robusta," has a thinner trunk than its "filifera" cousin. They look good in multiples to soften the height of three story homes on Pensacola Beach. Below the palms are clumps of pampas grass in fall bloom.

CALIFORNIA FAN PALM, WASHINGTON PALM
Scientific name: *Washingtonia filifera*
Hardy to: Zone 8a
Habit: Solitary, arborescent
Height to 40'+ Spread: to 10'
Color: Deep green
Leaf: Palmate (with slight fold)
Petiole: Armed with large, curved tooth-like projections
Salt tolerance: Moderate
Shade tolerance: Full sun
Origin: Baja California, Southern California
Somewhat more cold hardy than its cousin, *robusta,* but every bit as fast growing on the Gulf Coast. Its trunk can be massive, and frankly out of scale for some smaller yards. I planted a seven gallon specimen (about 3' tall) close to the sound in Gulf Breeze, Florida. Over the course of 15 years it has attained a height of 40', and the base of its trunk is 4' across! It exhibits only a slight lean due to the severe storm surge and 130 mph winds of Hurricane Ivan in 2004 which is a strong testament to the sheer strength of established palms in storms. Again, you may find palms in nurseries tagged as *robusta* or *filifera*, but most likely either is probably a combination of both.

California Fan Palm - A massive palm with a broad base. This specimen has its upper trunk naturally skirted with older fronds; a nice look for taller fan palms

CANARY ISLAND DATE PALM
Scientific name: *Phoenix canariensis*
Hardy to: Zone 8b
Habit: Solitary, arborescent
Height: to 40' Spread: to 25'+
Color: Medium green
Leaf: Pinnate
Petiole: Heavily armed with stiff, dagger-like spikes that morph into leaflets further up the frond
Salt tolerance: Moderate
Shade tolerance: Full sun
Origin: Canary Islands (duh!)

Often planted along the Gulf Coast, but more often than not in the wrong place, this very tropical (Mediterranean) looking specimen can not be planted any closer than 12' to 14' from anything else. It is truly a stand alone palm that must be given its space. The spectacular arching fronds can themselves be 12' to 14' long. It develops a massive trunk, also perhaps 3'+ in diameter. Pruning of the palm is simple, but many times done incorrectly. Always prune individual fronds close enough to the trunk so that no armaments remain. Otherwise, this friendly palm looks as though its trunk is wrapped in a crown of thorns.

Canary Island Date Palm requires a large space. This specimen has fern growing from its trunk. This does not harm the palm.

SILVER DATE PALM, INDIAN DATE PALM, TODDY PALM
Scientific name: *Phoenix sylvestris*
Hardy to: Zone 8b
Habit: Solitary, arborescent
Height: to 30' Spread: to 12'+
Color: Glaucous, silver, gray green
Leaf: Pinnate
Petiole: Heavily armed with long stiff spikes
Salt tolerance: Moderate
Shade tolerance: Full sun
Origin: India

Silver Date Palm

Since this more size manageable cousin of *canariensis* has a silvery appearance to its fronds, you might guess why it is called a silver date palm. Its trunk rarely exceeds 18" in diameter and many times has a striking orange hue to it. The fronds are usually only half the length of the *canariensis,* and are quite stiff and more upright. I understand that the sap was boiled down in India and fermented to create an alcoholic beverage. The British were fond of the warmed beverage and referred to it as a hot toddy. This palm has not been as widely sold or planted on the Gulf Coast as *canariensis,* but is probably more useful as a landscape focus because of its smaller size.

DATE PALM
Scientific name: *Phoenix dactylifera*
Hardy to: Zone 8b
Habit: Solitary, arborescent
Height: to 50'+
Spread: 25'+
Color: Olive green
Leaf: Pinnate
Petiole: Armed with sharp spikes
Salt tolerance: High
Shade tolerance: Full sun
Origin: North Africa

This palm is grown throughout Mideastern countries to produce edible dates, as well as for landscape purposes. I can't help but be reminded of its natural desert habit when I see them. Fewer plants look more out of place on the Gulf Coast than these very expensive stately centurions of drier climates. The only places we are seeing date palms to any extent on the Gulf Coast are at casinos, perhaps to make you think you are in the Las Vegas desert, and more recently at hospitals and healthcare facilities! Well, it just goes to show they have too much of our money. Before you decide to be first in your neighborhood to own a 20' to 40' "Medjool" (the preferred variety of *dactylifera*), know that you will have to pay upwards of $10,000 to have one installed.

Date Palms used to line entrance to a local hospital

The City of New Orleans which prides itself on its eclectic cultural ambiance has planted dozens of "Medjools" on both sides of Canal Street. This main commercial thoroughfare has the historic French Quarter on one side and Harrah's Casino on the other. "Laissez les bons temps rouler" (Let the good times roll).

Bismarckian nobilis or Bismarck Palm to left. Acoelorrhaphe wrightii or Paurotis Palm to right. We do see these palms on the gulf coast but either may be heavily damaged by our freezes.

TREES

Trees (and/or palms) should be foremost in your mind when planning your landscape. It is difficult for me to visualize a landscape without first determining the locations and selection of trees. Only then do I know what parts of the yard will receive sunshine and which parts will receive shade. I also cannot imagine anyone who has lived on the Gulf Coast through one of our summers that would not want parts of the yard to be shaded. Trees also cool the local environment in another way other than shading. As they transpire water vapor, the evaporation pulls heat from the surrounding area. Besides shading and cooling, trees are also planted for noise reduction (especially traffic), to attract wildlife (especially birds), and lastly for aesthetics.

There are trees that flower in the spring, those that flower in the summer, and those that flower in the fall. Even with no significant flowers, a well established, magnificent live oak can add thousands of dollars of value to a property. There is something that can be awe inspiring, peaceful and spiritual in the presence of a well loved tree.

The Gulf Coast can be divided into two zones for tree consideration. The first zone is within 20 miles of the coast, and the second zone is beyond that 20 mile zone. The first zone does not get as many chill hours as the second zone, and the wind events are of course much stronger within 20 miles of the coast. Thus, because of slightly longer dormancy, dogwoods, redbuds, apples, peaches, plums, flowering cherrys, crabapples, etc. will perform better in this zone away from the coast. Because of wind events, fast growing deciduous trees such as red maple, tulip poplar, sweetgum, sycamore, pecan, etc. will perform better in the more northern zone.

Of course, folks in the more northern zone will be more frequently disappointed in many palm or citrus species because of more extreme cold. Again, it is important to know your own microclimate.

My following list of trees is not meant to be all inclusive, or by any means exhaustive. There are probably hundreds of species of trees you could enjoy on the Gulf Coast. These are again some of my favorites.

Trees are also fun to climb! Exfoliating bark of Natchez Crape adds the fringe benefit of exceptional crimson color.

Ornamental Trees – less than 30', flowering

Crape Myrtle, *Lagerstroemia indica*, especially *fauriei* crosses
Indian Hawthorn Tree, *Raphiolepis indica*
Loblolly Bay, *Gordonia lasianthus*
"Little Gem" Magnolia, *Magnolia grandiflora*
Jerusalem Thorn, *Parkinsonia aculeata*
Dogwood, *Cornus florida* (may be difficult to establish closer to the coast)
Redbud, *Cercis canadensis*
Japanese or Saucer Magnolia, *Magnolia soulangiana, stellata, lilifora*
Ligustrum, *Ligustrum japonica, recurvifolia*
Chaste Tree, *Vitex* sp.

Crape Myrtle that is planted in front of my business. It is an example of my favorite fauriei cross, "Natchez"

Ornamental Trees – less than 30', No significant flowering

Japanese Maple, *Acer palmatum*
Trident Maple, *Acer buergerianum*
Japanese Black Pine, *Pinus thunburgiana*
Wax Myrtle, *Myrica cerifera*
Native Yaupon Holly, *Ilex vomitoria*
Italian Cypress, *Cypressus sempervirens*
Palms, Various

Japanese Maple - This beautiful specimen is one of the many green leaf varieties.

Gulf Coast Fall Color

Fall color in trees is something that is often sought by residents of the Gulf Coast. New residents from more northerly climates are especially insistent on choosing deciduous trees for their yards that produce the glorious reds and yellows that they remember from autumn in their home state. Luckily for us, many of these same trees that produce fall color in the southern Appalachians or even New York will grow here. The down side is our weather, which is inconsistent in the fall and winter. Our temperatures in October and November may be in the 30s or 80s. This inconsistent temperature is not conducive to the gradual, predictable coloring of the leaves, so fall color along the Gulf Coast is a rare event happening only every few years.

Take consolation in what the Gulf Coast offers – beautiful beaches, gracious southern towns and seaports, and outstanding fishing! We are a tourist destination for the entire world, but we will never become a destination resort known for beautiful fall color. Let us graciously concede that loss to New England, or towns along the Blue Ridge Parkway. However, the following four pictures were taken in December, 2009 right here on the Gulf Coast. They are excellent examples of a rare, but appreciated phenomenon, "Gulf Coast fall color."

Red Maple

Right - Bradford Pear
Bottom Left- Crape Myrtle
Bottom Right - Japanese Maple

Longleaf Pine is the state tree of Alabama. Prior to logging and development, the Longleaf Pine was the predominant forest tree along most of the Gulf Coast. It can be distinguished from its more common cousins, Slash Pine and Loblolly Pine, most easily by its larger cones, 6" to 10" and longer needles, 10" to 15" (always 3 to a bundle).

Pines, especially Slash and Longleaf are grossly under-rated and unappreciated as landscape trees. All too frequently new homeowners will want to remove native pines and scoff at the suggestion of planting pines as landscape trees. In fact, pines can create an ideal overstory for a beautiful yard. The filtered shade will not interfere with the growth of St. Augustine grass and will also allow azaleas, camellias, redbuds and other of our favorite shade loving plants to thrive.

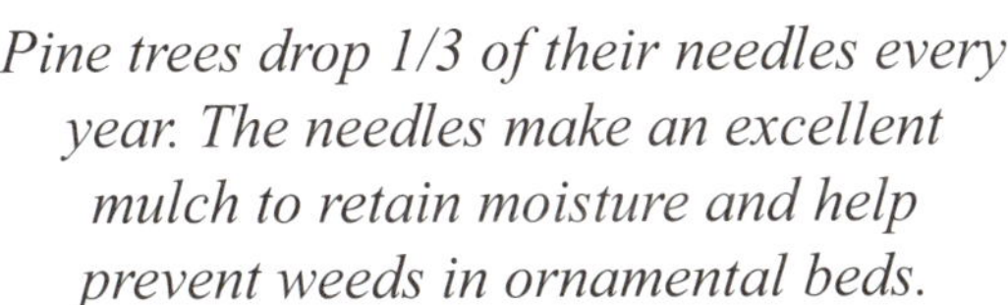

Pine trees drop 1/3 of their needles every year. The needles make an excellent mulch to retain moisture and help prevent weeds in ornamental beds.

Live Oak - It is obvious from the characteristic convoluted branching of this tree that it grew in a woodland situation, prior to the new home being built.

<u>Shade Trees 30' and up – Deciduous</u>

River Birch, *Betula nigra*
Red Maple, *Acer rubrum*
Sweetgum, *Liquidambar styraciflua*
Tulip Poplar, *Liriodendron tulipifera*
Sycamore, *Platanus occidentalis*
Pond Cypress, *Taxodium ascendens*
Bald Cypress, *Taxodium distichum*
"Muscogee" Crape Myrtle, *Lagerstromia indica x fauriei*
Blackgum, *Nyssa sylvatica*
Schumard Oak, *Quercus shumardii*
Sawtooth Oak, *Quercus acutissima*
Drake Elm, Alle Elm or Bosque Elm, *Ulmus parvifolia*
Bradford Pear, *Pyrus calleryana*

<u>Shade Trees 30' and up – Evergreen</u>

Live Oak, *Quercus virginiana*
Southern Magnolia, *Magnolia grandiflora*
Longleaf Pine, *Pinus palustris*
Slash Pine, *Pinus ellioti*
Holly, *Ilex (attenuata, cassine, cornuta)* (Savannah, Dahoon, Mary Nell, Nellie R. Stevens)
Sweetbay Magnolia, *Magnolia virginiana*
Deodar Cedar, *Cedrus deodora*
Eastern Red Cedar, *Juniperus virginiana*

Two Southern Magnolias are shown above. The one on the right is probably a seedling of native plants. It is already 60' tall and given the opportunity can grow larger still. The one on the left is a cultivated variety or cultivar known as "Little Gem." At 20' this specimen is close to its mature size. Southern Magnolia is the state tree of Mississippi. Please pass me a mint julep!

This Savannah Holly in New Orleans is evergreen and will produce red berries in the winter. Its smaller size should not overpower the home.

Above: The trees shading the statue with the trumpet are Bald Cypress. the state tree of Louisiana. These trees stand in a park in New Orleans that memorializes a native son, Louis Armstrong.

Above Right: River Birch is a light and airy multi-trunk shade tree. Some of the newer cultivars really show off a white bark that exfoliates periodically.

Right: Red Maple - A native along the gulf coast as well as most of the eastern United States. This picture exemplifies the reason for its name. In January or February they show off small red flowers which will give way to green leaves in the spring.

To Plant a Tree

Move the potted tree to a place in your yard that you are certain will give you years of enjoyment, as well as enjoyment to subsequent generations.

The newly acquired Bald cypress in this drawing is being planted in the lawn, so the first step is to remove the sod in a circle at least twice as wide as the pot. In this case the tree is in a 15 gallon size container which is 18" across. A circle of 36" of sod is removed.

Dig the hole for the root ball keeping the hole about the same shape as the pot, only make the hole several inches wider than the pot. In this case a 24" to 26" wide hole will suffice. Do not make the hole any deeper. As you dig the hole, place the soil you remove just to the edge of the hole in a uniform circle around the hole.

Now remove the plastic nursery pot from the root ball. Place the tree's root ball in the center of the hole. Make sure the top of the root ball is at the same level as the surrounding level of the ground. Make sure the tree is straight up and down. You may have to tilt the root ball somewhat to achieve this, but that's okay.

Have the hose out with you as you plant the tree. Put several inches of native soil back in the hole and wash it down with the hose to a soupy consistency. Re-straighten the tree if necessary.

Rake or shovel in several more inches of soil, and wash it down uniformly around the root ball. Repeat until the soil is level with the ground. Extra soil is now available around the previous hole, Rake it into a uniform, shallow berm just outside the root ball. Soil should not be added to the top of the root ball. This shallow berm will now hold water and direct its seepage directly on to the root ball.

Now use a natural wood mulch or pine needles to cover the 36" circle of berm and root ball. Be sure to place only an inch or so of mulch directly on the root ball, but it can be thicker, perhaps 2", on the berm. Pine straw can and should be thicker because it will settle over time. You should now fertilize your newly planted tree by spreading a balanced, slow release granular fertilizer evenly within the bermed area. Water in the fertilizer. You are now done. Walk around and admire the new addition to your landscape. Feel blessed!

Postscript - Newly planted trees need to be watered with a hose for several weeks or several months after installation. Sprinkler systems will not suffice until the tree is established. Consult your nurseryman for watering frequency and duration which will vary with soil types and the season of install.

MORE PLANT LISTS

The following lists are arranged according to how you might consider plants for particular landscape situations. They are all plants that I use to landscape with frequently, so they are plants that I have come to know and trust as to their durability and suitability in zone 8 and 9 conditions. While I have listed only the common names for ease and brevity, you should be careful picking the correct cultivars or varieties. Some size differences can surprise you.

The lists are again not meant to be all inclusive or exhaustive. Feel free to expand your horticultural horizons over time, perhaps experimenting with something you have observed or even a neighbor's recommendation.

If you find yourself developing an interest in a particular genre of plants, check out specific books or local clubs. Pensacola, Florida has rose societies, camellia clubs and even Hemerocalis (Daylily) societies.

Japanese Yew is a terrific screening plant. This was taken along St. Charles Avenue in New Orleans. The white washed brick posts and carefully pruned yew form a private courtyard along a well-traveled thoroughfare.

Plants to Consider for Screening, Privacy or tall hedges – 8' plus

Ligustrum
Hollies
Leyland Cypress
Arizona Cypress
"Little Gem" Magnolias
Azaleas, Southern Indica
Indian Hawthorn, "Majestic Beauty" or "Rosalinda"
Cleyera
Viburnum
Bottlebrush (cold sensitive)
Japanese Yew
Camellia sasanqua
Pampas Grass
Pittosporum
Blueberry, Rabbiteye
Oleander (cold sensitive)
Splitleaf Philodendron (cold sensitive)
Bamboo (clumping varieties)

Red Formosa Azalea - This particular plant is pruned into a patio tree 5'- 6' tall. It graces the fence between two spirea in my back yard.

Plants to Consider for Building Corners, can be maintained at 6' to 8'

Japanese Yew
Camellia japonica
Camellia sasanqua
Bottlebrush (cold sensitive)
Ligustrum
Cleyera

Plants to Consider to Accent a Wall 6' to 12'

Any of the above corner plantings are suitable plus the following.
Obelisk or Trellis with Jasmine, creeping fig or ivy
Sago
European Fan Palm
Needle Palm
Windmill Palm
Sky Pencil
Weeping Mulberry
Japanese Maple
Patio Rose Tree
Poodle or Spiral Juniper, Arizona Cypress or Ligustrum
Indian Hawthorn Tree
Weeping Yaupon
Azalea Tree, Southern Indica
Nandina domestica

Backyard Trees and Bushes with Edible Fruit

Peach, low chill hour variety, self fertile
Apple, low chill hour variety, requires pollinator
Pear, low chill hour variety, better production with pollinator
Loquat, self fertile
Fig, self fertile, closed eye variety
Oriental Persimmon, self fertile
Blueberry, rabbiteye varieties, better production with three or more pollinators
Mulberry, self fertile
Citrus, self fertile, especially more cold hardy varieties such as kumquat and satsuma
Olive, some varieties self fertile, others require pollinator

Kumquat - This particular specimen is a Meiwa Kumquat, slightly sweeter than the more oblong variety, Nagami. This is one of several cold hardy citrus varieties in my back yard.

Plants For a Low Focal Point Near Entrance

Sago
European Fan Palm
Pom Pom Juniper
Muhly Grass
A grouping of 3 "Knockout" Roses, or 3 Loropetalum

Plants That Are Consistent, Dependable, and Evergreen That Can Be Maintained at 2' – 4' as a Basic Foundation Planting

Dwarf Yaupon
Indian Hawthorn, compact varieties
Dwarf Pittosporum
Japanese Boxwood
Ilex crenata compacta
Delcambre Holly
Azaleas
Nandina, dwarf variety
Loropetalum, dwarf or compact variety

An unexpected flash of color from Plumbago along a screening wall.

Consistent Color During Warm Weather Without Replacement (possibly)

Plumbago (cold sensitive)
Tibouchina (cold sensitive)
Blue Daze (cold sensitive)
Bush Daisy (cold sensitive)
"Knockout" Roses
Bougainvillea (cold sensitive)
Lantana
Mexican Petunia (invasive)
Mexican Sage
Hibiscus (cold sensitive)
Mandevilla (cold sensitive)
"Encore" Azaleas
"Endless Summer" Hydrangeas

Backup, accents, and Plants With Motion

Splitleaf Philodendron (cold sensitive)
Ornamental grasses including Muhly, Miscanthus, Pennisetum, Paspalum
Agapanthus
African Iris
Foxtail Fern
Society Garlic
Aztec Grass
Evergreen Giant Liriope
Dianella

Plumbago - A prolific perennial bloomer. It will flower as long as it's warm and easily over winter in zone 9.

Groundcovers

Asiatic Jasmine
Blue Rug Juniper
Procumbens Nana Juniper
Mondo Grass
Liriopes
Creeping Periwinkle

Muhly Grass loves full sun and little water. In the fall it is fully resplendent with its almost cloud-like crimson inflorescence of plumes

Tibouchina in my back yard. It blooms as long as it is warm. It dies back in the winter and reflourishes in spring. In February I cut it back severely to about 2'. By summer's end, it is 6' tall.

<u>Vines</u>

Confederate Jasmine
Carolina Jessamine
Creeping Fig
Honeysuckle
Wisteria
Cross vine
Trumpet vine
Mandevilla (cold sensitive)
Bougainvillea (cold sensitive)
Lady Banks Rose

The porches on this New Orleans French Quarter home are flush with color from the bright pink Mandevilla. Hopefully it will make it through the winter.

Carolina Jessamine, a native on the upper gulf coast creeps over a fence from a wooded area. The blooms are seen in January and February.

Italian Cypress used to break up a plain, white block wall in Fairhope, Alabama.

Japanese Aucuba - This particular cultivar is "Gold Dust." These plants are robust and the yellow-green leaves are a great contrast in this shady environment.

Variegated Ginger is another great yellow-green foliage plant to break up green backgrounds. You can see the ginger in this partially shaded area peeking out from under an old Pittosporum.

Plants for Shaded Areas

Trees: Magnolia
Dogwood
Redbud
Japanese Maple
Windmill Palm

Shrubs: Azaleas
Camellia sasanqua
Camellia japonica
Hydrangeas
Pittosporum
Spiraea, "Bridal Wreath" and "Anthony Waterer"
Japanese Yew
Tea Olive, *Osmanthus fragrans*
Viburnum, *Odoratissimum* (large)
Cleyera
Aucuba, Japanese
Gardenias
Butterfly Bush
Splitleaf Philodendron (cold sensitive)
Ladyfinger Palm (cold sensitive)
Dwarf Palmetto
Needle Palm
Saw Palmetto
Sago

Others: Ferns, esp. Holly Fern, and many others
Gingers, esp. variegated
Asiatic Jasmine
Liriopes
Mondo Grass
Creeping Periwinkle
Hostas
Cast Iron Plant

Citrus trees not only produce abundant fruit in our warmer coastal areas, they can be quite ornamental. The dark green foliage of this orange tree really makes the white of this historic church stand out in Old Seville Square in Pensacola, FL.

This small shaded curbside bed features a cardboard palm (Zamia latifolia) surrounded by mondo grass. Pedestrians walking along the sidewalk on this Gulf Coast avenue will be pleasantly surprised by the unexpected patch of landscape.

Plants for Salt, Sand, Sun and Wind – Environments of Our Barrier Islands

Trees: Sand Live Oak
Magnolia
Jerusalem Thorn
Japanese Black Pine
Slash Pine
Eastern Red Cedar

Ligustrum
Indian Hawthorn tree
Palms, most cold hardy and wind tolerant species
Loquat, possibly
Fig, possibly
Olive, possibly

Shrubs: Indian Hawthorn, all varieties
Junipers, all forms
Dwarf Yaupon
Native Yaupon
Pittosporum, all varieties
Oleander, all varieties
Elaeagnus
Chaste tree, vitex
Japanese Yew
Century plant
Sago
Yucca
Agave

Others: Sea Oats
Saltmarsh Cord Grass
Sand Cord Grass
Pampas Grass
Muhly Grass
Miscanthus Grass
Dune Sunflower
Bush Daisies
Plumbago
Society Garlic

Note: Salt, sand, sun and wind tolerance for the plants listed is extremely variable depending on micro-climate and environment.

Sansanqua Camellia - This evergreen shrub blooms in late fall when few other plants are blooming.

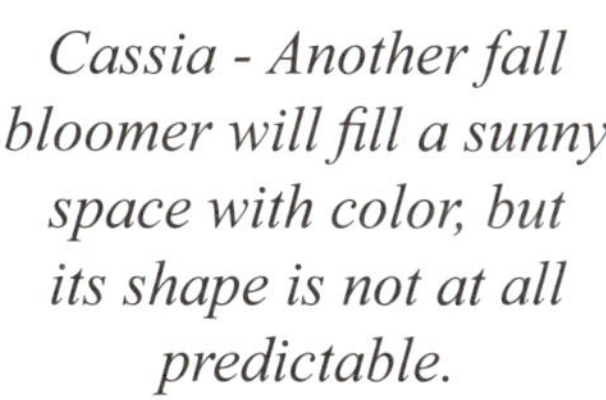

Cassia - Another fall bloomer will fill a sunny space with color, but its shape is not at all predictable.

This group of Bananas graces Jackson Square in New Orleans. While quite tropical looking, Banana plants can become scruffy looking after windy days or cold nights. Be ready to prune regularly.

"Knock Out" roses have been a hot item for the last few years. These lend their everblooming carefree color to an island bed in the East Hill section of Pensacola, FL.

The shade of large Live Oaks properly maintained, is an inviting respite in the hot southern sun. This large home in the New Orleans Garden District makes great use of its great oaks.

Vitex or Chaste Tree - Profuse bloomer late spring or summer. This specimen enhances the waterfront in Apalachicola, Florida

EPILOGUE

I think it is safe to say that 99% of my landscape clients ask for a low maintenance, or maintenance free landscape. I am forced to tell them that "maintenance free" is impossible on the Gulf Coast, unless you opt for plastic plants and solid concrete for mulch. A low maintenance landscape is attainable; a little pruning here and there, a small amount of weeding periodically, and a mulch refreshing seasonally.

I personally don't like to toil in my landscape, but I absolutely love to tinker with it. I occasionally prune when the season is right. I weed perhaps 10 weeds every week to keep the beds weed free, and in the fall I really enjoy raking pine needles off the lawn to spread under the beds of trees and shrubs. About once or twice a year I transplant one or several plants. I do all of this alone "one on one with Mother Nature", if you will. Working and shaping a landscape can be a spiritual experience.

I, for one, have not found God in the Bible or in church. I do feel a connection to God when I gaze into the night sky filled with galaxies, stars, planets and moons. And when I hear the songs of birds, the laughter of children, the wisdom of our elders, and the seas rush to shore, I detect the voice of God. I love to experience God's creation in deep quiet, old growth forests, or on the mountain tops of the southern Appalachians, and along many of the clear, spring fed streams of our area. And sometimes when the spring sun warms my skin on a cool day and the leaves and blooms are emerging from their winter's sleep, I am certain I see the face of God right in my own back yard as I tend my garden.

We come from the earth.

We return to the earth.

In between, we garden.

Author unknown

NOTES

NOTES

NOTES

NOTES

NOTES

THE GULF COAST LANDSCAPE

For additional copies call: 850-934-1043
OR
By mail: Mike's Garden
3774 Gulf Breeze Parkway
Gulf Breeze, Florida 32563

Name:____
Address:____
City:____________________**State:**________**Zip:**______________

Number of Copies x $29.95 ____________________
Plus shipping x $4.00 ea. ____________________
Sales tax (FL residents only) 6.5% ____________________
TOTAL: $____________________

Please make checks payable to Mike's Garden

THE GULF COAST LANDSCAPE

For additional copies call: 850-934-1043
OR
By mail: Mike's Garden
3774 Gulf Breeze Parkway
Gulf Breeze, Florida 32563

Name:____
Address:____
City:____________________**State:**________**Zip:**______________

Number of Copies x $29.95 ____________________
Plus shipping x $4.00 ea. ____________________
Sales tax (FL residents only) 6.5% ____________________
TOTAL: ____________________

Please make checks payable to Mike's Garden

ALABAMA
MISSISSIPPI
LOUISIANA
WASHINGTON
TANGIPAHOA
ST. TAMMANY
HANCOCK
HARRISON
JACKSON
MOBILE
MOBILE
BILOXI
LAKE PONTCHARTRAIN
NEW ORLEANS
ORLEANS
ST. JOHN
ST. CHARLES
JEFFERSON
ST. BERNARD
PLAQUEMINES
GULF